Discerning Inclusion

Discerning Inclusion

How an Evangelical Church Had
the Conversation about LGBT+ Inclusion

ASHLEY HARDINGHAM

Foreword by David P. Gushee

RESOURCE *Publications* • Eugene, Oregon

DISCERNING INCLUSION
How an Evangelical Church Had the Conversation about LGBT+ Inclusion

Resource Publications
An Imprint of Wipf and Stock Publishers
199 W. 8th Ave., Suite 3
Eugene, OR 97401

www.wipfandstock.com

PAPERBACK ISBN: 979-8-3852-1393-1
HARDCOVER ISBN: 979-8-3852-1394-8
EBOOK ISBN: 979-8-3852-1395-5

07/30/24

Dedicated with love and respect
to the Altrincham Baptist Church family.

In necessariis unitas, in dubiis libertas, in omnibus caritas.

Contents

Foreword by David P. Gushee   ix

Preface   xiii

Acknowledgments   xvii

Introduction   xix

1   Precipitation—how the conversation came about   1

2   The Tipping Point   14

3   Devising the Process   25

4   Starting the Process   35

5   What do our Church Members Think?   46

6   Handling Critiques and Criticisms   54

7   How (Baptist) churches do doctrinal difference   68

8   Concluding the Process   78

9   What the Church Discerned   91

10 Counting the Cost (and Reaping the Benefits)   100

11 Reflecting on the Process   112

Postscript   114

Bibliography   119

Foreword

IN MUCH OF THE world, Christian churches are entering into difficult discernment processes related to the controversial question of LGBT+ inclusion. Discernment is the right word, as Ashley Hardingham argues in this careful description of the thoughtful process in which he led his Altrincham Baptist Church (ABC) on its way toward full inclusion.

For Christians, the word discernment connotes a quest to obtain God's guidance, to learn God's will, in relation to a major decision we face. Discernment is not just finding out facts or drawing wise conclusions by making use of our human rational capacities. It is instead a spiritual process, a being-led-by-God (we hope) toward what is good, right, true, and best, toward what pleases God and is fitting for followers of Jesus Christ.

Most days, most of the time, most Christians and churches don't need to enter elaborate discernment processes. Our long-standing traditions, habits, and convictions seem to provide all that we need to engage with current challenges and decisions. That is a gift, really, because discernment processes are difficult and exhausting undertakings for their participants, and high-risk ventures for pastors and churches.

There is a clue hiding in that last paragraph that may help explain a few things that you will encounter in the pages to follow. You will see, for example, that certain members of ABC opposed the very idea of a discernment process related to LGBT+ inclusion. Some opposed it so profoundly that they left the church before it yielded any results. The process itself was offensive to them.

Perhaps this signals something: the very decision to enter a discernment process in a church reflects the prior decision (or intuition, feeling, nudge) on the part of a church leader or leadership group that existing traditions, habits, and convictions do not in fact provide all that is needed in facing a particular issue. This means that for these leaders, a major question, issue, or area of life has become unsettled. New reflection, new discernment, is needed. But resistance to this idea then emerges intuitively, and immediately, from people who do not agree that existing traditions, habits, and convictions need reconsideration.

In other words, even the decision to enter a discernment process is, in fact, a matter of discernment. I have discerned that we need some discernment, says the pastor. But at least when it comes to discernment processes related to LGBT+ inclusion, there always appear to be congregants who do not agree that the longstanding rejectionist posture of the church needs any reconsideration. And they fear, perhaps with good reason, that if pastors or leadership are initiating a discernment process, their very sense that such a process is needed may signal the likely outcome of the process— however long, careful and elaborate it might be.

All that being said, as an advocate of full LGBT+ inclusion in the churches, I am all in—not just for discernment processes, but for the kind of very careful, very measured, step-by-step process that Pastor Ashley Hardingham describes in this book. In my experience, such processes never, ever, bring consensus. They always, always cost the church members and money, at least in the short term. But they often produce gains in significant goods for Christian life—in depth and quality of Bible study and moral reflection, in practices of communal conversation, and in the church's LGBT+ members having the opportunity to speak their truths, to tell their stories, usually for the very first time.

As well, the more transparent, fair, and democratic the discernment process in a congregation, the more likely it is that even congregants who remain uncertain about the substance of matters related to LGBT+ discernment will at least agree that the process was respectful and just. In other words, as a matter of polity, especially but not exclusively in congregationalist settings, careful discernment processes reinforce the democratic and covenantal norms of the church community. That is not a small matter.

Discerning Inclusion is one of only a handful of books on the recent surge of church discernment processes related to LGBT+ inclusion. Especially if you are a pastor, leader or church member in a church that is heading down this road, you need not just to read but to study every one of the pages that follow.

DAVID P. GUSHEE
Distinguished University Professor of Christian Ethics,
Mercer University, USA
Chair in Christian Social Ethics, Vrije Universiteit, Amsterdam

Preface

THIS IS NOT A book about ethics, theology, or biblical exegesis. I'm not attempting to describe or define the morality of same-sex relations, seeking to create a theological framework to understand them, or adding my take to the plethora of competing (and conflicting) claims authors have regarding what the Bible *"actually"* says on the issue. This is a book about leadership. It is a book for ministers, church leaders, and any other interested parties about leading a church through a process, a conversation about discernment regarding LGBT+ inclusion. Whilst I am a Baptist minister, and therefore one whose discernment and decision-making processes are congregational, my hope is that there will be much in this book which might resonate with those leading churches in many denominations and affiliations who wish to engage with this issue.

As such, my intention in writing this book is to describe the process one evangelical church took to discern its view on LGBT+ inclusion. We dared to have the conversation and we learned a lot along the way. We learned about what information and content we might employ, and about what stages would constitute a full and thorough process. We learned about how culture can shape our views. We also learned a lot about ourselves, about how we relate, listen and speak to each other, especially on a subject which seems to incite such varied and passionate responses. We probed and reflected on what spiritual discernment is, how we understand developments or changes to our beliefs and how we might attend to the Holy Spirit as He guides us. And as a church leader, I learned much about how to lead a church through the choppy and rock-strewn waters of discussing one of the most pressing and defining issues for the church today: in what way should we welcome, and potentially accept and include those from the LGBT+ communities in church life?

Most of the long-standing denominations—Anglicans, Roman Catholics, URC and Methodist churches—determine their views centrally. After all, these denominations are broadly episcopalian in nature, meaning that they operate top-down governance, relying on bishops and synods to determine orthodoxy, and their practices across the whole church. Baptist churches and many in the "new church" tradition don't operate in that way. They are much more likely to use either a congregational model where the church members decide, or a presbyterian model where the church leadership team determines the church's view on the matter.

Clearly, the episcopal and presbyterian models deliver each congregation from having to undertake a discernment process in a way which involves everyone in the church. In this sense, it can often be a shorter and possibly simpler process. But many church leadership teams of either type will want to adopt a process whereby they involve the whole church family in gathering to discern the issue. This is what we did for just over a year. And this is the story of how we did it.

But before I embark on telling you what happened, just a word about language—something we found to be important. There is, I think, a lot of loose language around this issue, loose language which breeds ambiguity and uncertainty, but can equally be used to manipulate and control, so I have tried to be as clear as possible about the terms I use and what I mean by them. I have also had to decide exactly which words or phrases I will regularly use in the book. Whilst there are various acronyms used for those who are part of the lesbian, gay, bisexual, transgender, or queer communities (LGBTQ, LGBTQ+, LGBTQIA+), I have chosen to use LGBT+ throughout the book. I also use the word *inclusion*, by which I mean the inclusion of all LGBT+ people in welcome, acceptance, and involvement in church life. Such churches are often referred to as *affirming churches*.

Finally, I have used the word *discernment* in the title of the book, meaning *the ability to judge well*. Discernment is a word which is helpful in describing how God's leaders and people, in attending to God's word and the Holy Spirit, are able to determine together what God is saying. Inclusion is an eminently biblical idea. This is not because of its repeated use in the pages of Scripture,[1] but because it touches on the very heart of God who loves the whole world,[2] and whose desire is that none should perish.[3] The Bible's story is of the God whose call of Abraham, and Israel, then Gentiles, and which then reaches to the ends of the earth, demonstrates an ever-expanding incorporation of humanity, and indeed calls each who has come to know him to share the gospel with others. I also use the word *process* to describe what we did, as it indicates that there were certain stages which we undertook in order to discern. Although some speak of an inclusion *journey*, I have used discernment process in preference to journey. One thoughtful church member, who admittedly opposed the process we undertook, explained that he was "in no way going on a journey," something which implied from the outset that he had predetermined the destination he would arrive at. I understand and respect this view and therefore use the word process to describe what we did.

1. The word "inclusion" appears just once in NIV and NRSV Bibles, in Rom 11:12.

2. John 3:16.

3. 2 Pet 3:9.

Acknowledgments

IN THE EARLIEST STAGES of my exploration and questioning of the subject of this book it was Nik and Justin whose vulnerability and generosity in sharing their personal stories which helped deliver me from false perceptions and clarified my understanding. They took me from the realm of assumption and speculation to the cool and sometimes harsh reality of life lived as a gay, Christian man. In the same manner Isabelle, Elaine, Jim and Jackie were those who entrusted me with stories from their own families.

David Mayne, Dave Steell, Stephen Elmes, and Mike Parker are all Baptist ministers who have trod this path ahead of me and whose sagacious advice spared me many a fall.

I am very grateful to Keith and Karen Parr in whose Dylan Thomas esque Carradale shed, most of the book was written.

Justin, Nick Webb and Jan Webb, undertook the onerous task of reading the text with a view to correcting any unhelpful or inappropriate language. They also made numerous observations which honed my logic and clarified my writing.

I would also wish to acknowledge and thank those who encouraged me in this endeavor, but whom I cannot name because their association with this book would cause an unhelpful strain on their reputations and in their places of work. I similarly acknowledge without names, those members of my congregation and minister friends who hold a different view to mine and yet are still able to engage in discussion with equanimity, fair-mindedness and even a wry smile. May your exceptional character and attitude increasingly become the norm.

ACKNOWLEDGMENTS

My family, far from being spectators of the story this book tells, were all involved in it ever becoming a reality. I acknowledge the role that my daughters Zoe, Freya and Grace have played. My children can speak to me more directly than any minister, elder, or church member and with far great candor and daring due to the love we have for each other. It was they who first challenged my thinking and their persistence is surefire evidence that it does indeed take a family to raise a dad. And to my wife, thank you the most. Sandra endured the unique strain of supporting me through this journey. Our wedding vows were worked out through this process, for the burden of concern for another is often greater than the burden one might carry for oneself. And to my mother Andrea, who first shared with me the faith which I claim as my own and whose example is testimony to the openness, wisdom and understanding which can still define later life.

Publishing a book requires several different skills and disciplines, many of which I do not possess. So I am grateful to Jean Morgan whose eagle eyes pored over the text, and whose revisions mean that the reader will be spared my many literary iniquities. Also, Sheila Jump's skills in Microsoft and all things I.T. more than made up for my deficits in this field. As my church well knows, everyone needs a Sheila.

Finally, I would like to express my gratitude to Matt Wimer and the team at Wipf & Stock for taking me on; even as one of Brueggemann's 'uncredentialed ones'.

Introduction

How on earth do you lead an evangelical church through the conversation about LGBT+ inclusion? That was the question facing me the morning after the church elders had entrusted me with coming up with just such a process. Usually in church life there is for leaders some kind of roadmap, some textbook or guidance on an issue, which admittedly might need adapting, but would at least provide a template for how to guide the church through an issue. But not, it seems, on this one.

Yet the emergence of the issue of LGBT+ inclusion in society as one of the most pressing issues is now making the church face up to it as well. Society has, in the main, already determined its mind on the matter. Full inclusion of those in LGBT+ communities is now the norm in education, retail, and the corporate world, and it is now generally accepted that your local supermarket, council, and high street bank will be celebrating Pride Week with rainbow flags and banners. This has brought the church, even us the evangelical church, to a place of sober reflection. Hitherto, the evangelical church has been the place where the question of LGBT+ inclusion has been viewed by many as a non-question. Just move on, there is nothing to talk about here.

But the issue is not so easily brushed away, and now even *we* are talking about it. Some have viewed this as the ground on which the battle for evangelical orthodoxy is to be won or lost, and fiercely defend the traditional view. On this issue, fearing that all may be lost, some threaten schism or at least disfellowshipping those who give airtime to the subject. Others have been slower to defend the traditional view, seeing this as a contemporary issue which necessarily requires examination, and as such have made space for questions and even the proffering of an alternative view.

The truth is that ministers from whichever denomination have talked about the issue for many years. In almost thirty years of Baptist ministry, I have attended numerous day seminars or ministers' gatherings where the issue has been addressed directly or at least touched upon—gatherings which are almost always prefaced by the announcement that "What's said in this room, stays in this room." This is indicative of the significant level of fear which the issue excites amongst evangelical church leaders. It's one thing to have the conversation on a Thursday morning amongst colleagues, but quite another to have it on a Thursday evening amongst your church members, let alone in a Sunday service.

There is a huge amount of fear around the question of LGBT+ inclusion in evangelical churches. Fear about the possibility of changing one's mind on an issue about which there has been broad and certain agreement for centuries. Fear amongst church congregations that people will leave the church over this matter. And fear especially amongst church leaders that your evangelical identity is now defined by what your take is on this particular issue.

EVANGELICAL YES, BUT . . .

This book's title identifies the church I have served and ministered in for the past twelve years, as an *evangelical* church. So, what does that mean? After all, within the 2,000-year history of the church, the term "evangelical" is a relatively recent addition to its lexicon. And then of course there are various flavors of evangelicalism. There are those who wish to own the title *conservative* evangelical, whereas some are *mainstream* evangelicals. Similarly, there are those who call themselves *broadly* evangelical and dare I say, some who see themselves as *left-field* evangelical. However, all these descriptions include the word evangelical, about which we need to gain some clarity.

Rather than devise my own definition of the word, something which we evangelicals are only too keen to do, it strikes me as being more helpful to appeal to a long-held and widely recognized definition of the word. When looking for such, a Baptist colleague, Mark Elder, helpfully points to the work of David Bebbington. Still in print, Bebbington's *Evangelicalism in Modern Britain: A History from the 1730s to the 1980s* identifies four defining characteristics of what it is to be a (British) evangelical—what is termed the Bebbington quadrilateral. In short, these characteristics are conversionism, activism, biblicism, and crucicentrism. Whilst these elements might at first appear to be self-explanatory, it is worth giving them greater definition in order to ensure that there is no uncertainty when understanding Bebbington's quadrilateral.

Conversionism is the belief that human beings need to be converted in response to what Jesus has done. This is outworked especially through a call to conversion through evangelism and preaching. This brings to mind the words of my homiletics tutor at Spurgeon's College, London, who, perhaps overstating it somewhat, would encourage us young preachers to "quote the text and then head for Jesus." Activism is belief that the gospel needs to be expressed in activity and effort. Today, we may be more inclined to use the word activism when associating with *social* activism, but the word had a different emphasis for our nineteenth- century forebears. Activism, as they expressed it, was associated with their zeal for evangelism and preaching the gospel. Biblicism is the recognition of the authority of the Bible for all matters relating to faith (e.g., all essential spiritual truth is to be found in its pages). However, there was precious little analysis of Scripture in terms of more contemporary theologies of infallibility or inerrancy. The early evangelicals did not develop a doctrine of Scripture but were focused solely on the use of the message and story of the Bible as a means to develop discipleship, holiness, and witness. Finally, crucicentrism is the central importance of the atoning work of Jesus on the cross to save people from their sins. For eighteenth-century evangelical John Wesley, this was the doctrine on which all others rested, and it rightly differentiates Deism from Christianity.

It's interesting that whilst these terms give shape and meaning to what it is to be an evangelical, they remain broad, certainly broader than some would like. For example, Bebbington speaks of having a particular regard for the Bible and a belief that within its pages all spiritual truth can be found. But how is that reverence for the Bible discerned? Is it to be read literally? Is the meaning set and unchanging, or can it morph and develop over time with developments in science, textural criticism, or culture? Those are questions for you to answer, but Bebbington does offer us a reliable and sensible definition of the word. Where I think confusion arises is when the word evangelical is simply used as shorthand for conservative evangelical. Perhaps this is confusing—or maybe it is a bit of naughtiness by those who claim that their fundamentalist leanings are the only 'true' version of evangelicalism on offer.

ABC, A LOCAL CHURCH

My church, Altrincham Baptist Church (ABC), has had a long and evidently successful history as an evangelical church. Although it is difficult to discern the exact theological stance of the church stretching back to its origins in 1872, the early records of church life do indeed demonstrate attention to the word of God, outreach to the community and the importance of faith commitments and baptisms. Since the 1970s, the senior leaders have all been clear about their evangelical credentials and ministerial approach. The church saw significant growth in the 1970s under Paul Beasley-Murray, something which was sustained in the 1980s under Justin Dennison. Then in the 1990s and 2000s, under the leadership of Nigel Wright and Roger Sutton, the church continued to demonstrate these characteristics. ABC pioneered Chicago church Willow Creek's "Seeker Services," hosted Channel 4's filming of the Alpha Course and later briefly opened a nightclub, Ascension, in Manchester's Northern Quarter to engage with the clubbing scene. More recently, the church took on a large council-owned community building, The Hub, through which it has successfully developed many community activities. The Hub developed new means of community engagement during the Covid-19 pandemic when it became a key deliverer of services to the community. Today Sunday services are largely shaped around the teaching series, usually books of the Bible, and the church is charismatic in conviction and practice. Conversion and baptism remain core to our calling.

ABC is probably a mainstream evangelical church, by which I mean that within the gamut of evangelical prefixes we recognize and practice Bebbington's quadrilateral, but our teaching and theology also attracts those who are at both the conservative and the broad ends of the spectrum. But more of that later.

MY STORY

I was born in 1965 when homosexual acts between men were still illegal. (Whilst no British law has ever stated that lesbian acts between women have been illegal, there have still been prosecutions of women engaged in lesbian acts.[1]) Admittedly, by 1965, support for the recommendation of the Wolfenden Report of 1957 that "homosexual behavior between consenting adults in private should no longer be a criminal offence"[2] was gathering momentum. Even though the General Assembly of the Church of England agreed, ". . .. this Assembly generally approves the principles on which the criminal law concerned with sexual behavior should be based as stated by the Wolfenden Committee, and also its recommendations relating to homosexuality," the then Archbishop of Canterbury Geoffrey Fisher stated that, "I don't see the Christian Church ever giving its blessing to a marriage between persons of the same sex. The Church gives its blessing to the best and perfect use of sex, which is the union of a man and a woman in marriage. We confine our blessing to that."[3] Two years after my birth, the Sexual Offences Act, 1967, was passed, decriminalizing

1. Derry, *Lesbianism and the criminal law of England and Wales*, lines 20–23.
2. Wolfenden, *Report of the Committee on Homosexual Offences and Prostitution*, 115.
3. Willett, *Archbishops Fisher and Ramsey, and the Wolfenden Report*, lines 5–8.

homosexual acts between men if the following three criteria were met: the act had to be consensual, it had to take place in private and the act could involve only people who had attained the age of twenty-one. Society and its laws were changing, but slowly and with great caution. The church looked on with a mixture of biblical concern and pastoral understanding.

I have always gone to church. Throughout my childhood, Sundays were taken up with getting dressed up in my Sunday best and church early. There always seemed to be a reason for this: my parents' involvement in the service, to set out the chairs, or to hand out the green *Baptist Hymn Book* as people arrived. There was the service, Sunday School, refreshments, and rushing home to check on the Sunday lunch to which people were inevitably invited. We would then be back again in the evening, when I and my siblings became old enough to sit through another service.

This world was characterized by a heady and all-consuming mix of evangelical theology, practice, and culture. These were the times of *God's Smuggler*, of the Christian West bringing the light of God's word to the dark and iron-curtained East, and where *The Cross and the Switchblade* showed how the power of the gospel could even reach into the hearts of the least, the last, and the lost on the crime-ridden streets of New York. It was the heyday of Hal Lindsay's *Late Great Planet Earth*, the pre-millennial roadmap of how the world will end, with rapture followed by 1,000 years of Satan's rule. It was a theological perspective canonized in Cliff Richard's rendition of Larry Norman's terrifying vision, "I wish we'd all been ready." I have spoken to other children of the sixties and seventies who can also recall returning home from school to find mother absent and sense a rising fear that perhaps it was us who had been left behind.

These were the days of Keep Sunday Special, of stickers on Bibles and of grandparents' homes where the television set remained off on a Sunday. It was also the time when my parents went up to London to see Andrew Lloyd-Webber and Tim Rice's *Jesus Christ Superstar*. I remember listening to the cassette tape of the show and being mildly confused that, although the musical was all about the Jesus who was crucial to our family's identity, he was being depicted in terms which seemed oddly contemporary and, to my ears at least, potentially blasphemous.

In essence, the Christian environment in which I grew up drew stark lines between good and evil, God and the devil, right and wrong, what was sacred and what was secular. You were either for God or against him, and if Baptist minister Nigel Wright is correct in his view that the church should both "co-opt and contradict the world," there seemed to be an awful lot of contradicting and very little co-opting. So perhaps it wasn't surprising that, at the age of thirteen, I found myself accepting Christian faith for myself. In the spring of 1978, along with the church youth group, I attended Dick Saunders' Way to Life rally at Wembley Arena. With my mind in overdrive, listening to him define faith in all the ways with which I had become familiar, I heard the appeal to "get up out of my seat" and walk down to the front. But nerves and embarrassment held me back.

It wasn't until a few months later, in the first week of June, that I found myself in a Southern Baptist Convention church in Rota, southern Spain. We were on a family holiday and had decided to attend the American church linked to the nearby US air base. I remember that the message contained the challenge that "you are not a Christian just because your parents are." I recall that I was emotional and went out to the foyer of the church to speak to my dad about faith and what was going on inside me. Then, having returned to the service, the pastor gave an appeal to "walk the aisle" at which point I did, only to find my brother Tim appearing beside me a few moments later. We were, much to our grandmother's dismay as she would have loved to have been there, both baptized half an hour later. Imaginatively the baptistery had a painting of the Holy Land on both the back wall and front panel of the pool, so it appeared that in baptism we were descending into, and ascending from, the very waters of the Jordan.

Even in my mid- to late teens, this great divide between good and evil held sway. I have fond memories of waking up on a Sunday morning to the sound of my father banging out a tune on the piano downstairs. Although he couldn't sight-read, dad could pick out a tune and would play with great gusto the old Jim Reeves's song, "This World is not my Home," as a reveille to the day, with its underlying premise that life on earth is temporary, uncomfortable, and problematic, and that only the life to come will provide any peace, comfort, and meaningful existence.

These are fond memories, because it's my dad, and the tune registers on the soundtrack of those years, but the theology the song contains I have long since rejected. It encapsulated the dualism of the time—the great sacred/secular divide that was fundamental to the evangelical mindset, where the narrow gate and broad way of Matthew chapter 7 seemed to be the definitive text.

Whilst keeping us sharp and alert to temptation and sin, this mindset was less discerning when it came to applying welcome and grace to all people. In this respect, we aped the times and demonstrated little difference in our attitudes toward non-white people and homosexuals. We imbibed the casual racism of "The Black and White Minstrel Show" and the comedy of the time, along with the deprecation of effeminate behavior. So, the conversation around the Sunday lunch table would readily shift from assessing the merit of the sermon to the racism and homophobia present in the culture of those times in the jokes and humor we shared.

The consequence of these formative years was to leave me with "black-and-white" certainty regarding what was right and Christian, and what was wrong and ungodly. My Christian upbringing is something I treasure, and I consider myself immensely blessed to have received. It is where I learned the Bible and how to list all sixty-six books, and where I became familiar with its great characters and the overarching story. I was confronted with Jesus who in his love and grace died for me, even me. I was taught about the importance of giving and hospitality, and I gained a deep love for the church, amongst many other valuable lessons. It also developed in me the conviction that being a homosexual was wrong, and so wrong that it was unquestioningly wrong. I also had not the slightest shred of perception that there might be any difference between homosexual orientation and practice. So, at school, any boy who demonstrated non-masculine traits would be fair game for what we would now call homophobic abuse. And in church, the subject was hardly ever referenced; so far beyond the pale was it, that it required no further examination and was only mentioned when listed amongst the various sins in occasional Old and New Testament readings.

EARLY ENGAGEMENTS WITH FAITH AND LGBT+

It was during my time in a suburban London church while training for Baptist ministry that I first had to examine my own view on the matter. One of the young people came out to me and so, being an evangelical church of a conservative nature, the guidance from the senior leader was to contact the conservative Christian organization, True Freedom Trust. I did, and though I demonstrated concern for the young man, I now view my engagement with him as awkward and clunky. I dutifully passed on the material I had been sent and saw no reason not to toe the party line.

It wasn't until the "Noughties" and now leading a new church plant in north Leeds that I revisited the issue. Chapel A (a Baptist church) was a church comprised mainly of thirty- and forty-somethings with growing families. We were passionate about our engagement with community and culture, so it was of little surprise that at some point we looked at the issue. I spoke one Sunday, giving a broadly traditional view of same-sex relations, whereby my concession was that whilst orientation was not in itself sinful, participation in same-sex acts was wrong. After I had spoken, I invited an older couple to share the story of how with great love and care they engaged with their gay son and his gay Christian friends through his late teens and adult life. However, at the end of the service, controversy arose when another member, whose brother was gay, stood to share an impromptu alternative and inclusive Christian perspective on the subject. There seemed to be more to the issue than I had previously considered.

I followed the call from north Leeds to south Manchester in 2011: a move west along the M62 corridor and to a larger and much more established church, one which had experienced some recent tensions. Here was a church with more conservative inclinations. During the interview process, I was asked in a Q&A with the whole church whether I would "preach hell." I spluttered something about preaching hell in proportion to how much it appears in Scripture and, whilst gaining the support of most, this member and his wife left soon after my arrival. I wasn't once asked about my view of same-sex relations, and neither did I proffer one. After all, having recently negotiated some choppy waters, the church was, it seemed, just as concerned with finances, attendance, and membership numbers as it was with mission, teaching, and pastoral care. ABC was not a church which was likely to reconsider its traditional view of LGBT+ inclusion anytime soon.

1

Precipitation—how the
conversation came about

BACKSTORY

I CAME TO ABC in September 2011. It was then a large church
with a rich and impressive history. It was, some said, a church for
the region, a flagship Baptist church and at first, I had been unsure
of my ability to take on such a role. Two previous ministers had
left the church to take up the position of Principal at Spurgeon's
College in London, and I would be inheriting a large staff team
stretched across two buildings.

However, its most recent history had been a little shaky and
without saying as much, the expectation (mantle) being placed on
my shoulders felt pretty much like I was called to restore the for-
tunes of the church. Looking back, those first twelve months were
chaotic, as the fallout from what had been going on continued.
There were high-profile resignations of key posts in the church.
The Assistant Minister, Children's Minister, and CAP Centre Manager all stepped down, as did the church's Treasurer and Secretary.
Everyone wanted my ear, and it seemed that my working days were

spent listening to people and helping them to do their jobs, so at 5pm when others left for home, I started doing my own work.

The Leadership Team (elders) meetings were nervy and bureaucratic. Although never previously a fan of management books, I read Patrick Lencioni's *Five Dysfunctions of a Team*, especially employing the idea that I needed to be vulnerable to help restore the sense of trust that the church was so desperately lacking. So, eldership meetings were banned, at least for a few months, until I could speak to each elder privately, ascertain what the problems were and present them back to the eldership in order that we could start working on them together. I was under pressure to come up with a solution and come up with it fast, but God in his generosity gifted me some time to slow the process. On a visit to a day conference at Philadelphia Church in Sheffield, Paul Maconochie opened by referring to his Bible reading that morning, citing Proverbs 20:21, and suggested that this verse was God's words to one or more of those attending the day: "An inheritance claimed too soon will not be blessed at the end." I grabbed this with both hands and over the ensuing weeks recited it back to people repeatedly.

ABC was something of a super-tanker, and turning things around would both be difficult and time-consuming. It was very centralized in its activity. Experienced ministers were paid well to present well, lead well, and put on great services and evangelistic events. But in doing so, it felt that we were disarming and de-skilling the congregation. I wanted to animate and release each person to be a witness, a "minister" in their own right. I wanted to turn the spotlight from the minister on the platform to the member in the "pew."

When there is a big budget, a big staff team, a broad and complicated range of ministries, and a hefty reputation, the temptation will exist to simply focus on sustaining all this activity, whatever the cost. This can become a heavy burden and cruel master. Whether we like it or not, the numbers game is still played in the Christian world, with attendance, membership, budgets, and baptisms all cited as markers of success. So, when I arrived, it was still the task of one steward to count the people attending each Sunday, lest numbers decline. Although not verbalized, the sense was that you should avoid any actions or issues which might upset the status quo and knock the tanker off course. So, play it safe, keep people onside and play the game which would enable the church to regain its reputation and keep its numbers. After all, there are a lot of good churches in South Manchester and consumerism, which is one of the characteristics of this community, has ecclesiological implications as well.

I found those early years very demanding. I was being stretched by things beyond my previous experience and probably competence. I had no roadmap to follow but was simply trying to respond with wisdom based on those Christian values which I had come to know as being true and valuable in God's kingdom. Honesty, trustworthiness, gratitude—these things are non-negotiables in the church and slowly, very slowly, we seemed to change course and steady the ship. We began to write a different story for the church which was about the members and their lives.

THE POWER OF THE STATUS QUO

Occasionally matters arose which did challenge the status quo of a large, evangelical, charismatic(ish) church like ABC. One member challenged me about not being a Zionist, saying I had a "replacement theology" she was unhappy with. She left the church. Then one of my members who occasionally preached asked me about the passage he had been given to speak from. It was 1 Timothy 1 and included verses 9 and 10: "This means understanding that the law is laid down not for the innocent but for the lawless and disobedient, for the godless and sinful, for the unholy and profane, for those who kill their father or mother, for murderers, fornicators, sodomites, slave-traders, liars, perjurers, and whatever else is contrary to the sound teaching." His question was about "sodomites" and whether as a church we had a view on homosexuality. I hesitated slightly in my response, but composed myself and said that while we had no official position, we would uphold the church's traditional teaching that homosexual practice was not condoned.

3

Looking back, that slight hesitation was most likely a combination of momentarily wondering whether this was a moment to address this question, and my subconscious knowledge that we needed to keep everyone on board and not rock this boat.

It was then a preaching series through the book of Ephesians in spring 2018 which provided the single thread that I began to pull at, which ultimately unraveled with so many implications.

PERSONAL REVELATION

Some years previously, I had been urged by a church member to look at Ephesians as it was the book, they said, which was par excellence about the nature of the church. Eventually we got round to doing it. We are all familiar with the conversion of St Paul on the road to Damascus and then, as he writes in Galatians 1, his post- conversion journey to Arabia, back to Jerusalem and then finally to Jerusalem three years later. It is a journey, Tom Wright[1] suggests, which was all about Paul's immense brain trying to reconcile the truth he knew about the Law with the truth he had come to know about the resurrected Jesus Christ. One of the conclusions he reaches is about how God's grace and welcome now extended beyond Israelites, the chosen people of God, to the Gentile, the non-Jew. Chapter three of Ephesians seemed to be especially rich in exploring this new dimension to God's work.

> This is the reason that I Paul am a prisoner for Christ Jesus for the sake of you Gentiles. Eph 3:1

> . . . that is, the Gentiles have become fellow-heirs, members of the same body, and sharers in the promise in Christ Jesus through the gospel. Eph 3:6

> Although I am the very least of all the saints, this grace was given to me to bring to the Gentiles the news of the boundless riches of Christ. Eph 3:8

1. https://ntwrightpage.com/wp-content/uploads/2016/05/Wright_Paul_Arabia_Elijah.pdf

I'm unsure exactly why these passages of Scripture made such an impact on me. After all, I had heard many sermons (and doubtless preached a few) which would reference this shift. On all those occasions, I had noted this simply as a past event, an historical fact which gives reason to why "us Gentiles" are now invited into saving faith, and that reconciliation and peace with God was our experience too. But for some reason this had a huge impact on me. No longer was this a fact of the past, but it seemed to come alive in the present. It gave understanding to my experience today, that even I could experience God's warmth and welcome.

As an extrovert, I am, most probably, given to exaggeration and hyperbole, but even for me, this produced quite a response. I wanted to grab people by the lapels, look them deep in the eye and say, "Do you understand? The Gentiles . . . the Gentiles got welcomed into God's kingdom." And, if people were left in any doubt, I wanted to repeat, "THE GENTILES"! This was not simply for me a theological or biblical point which intrigued my intellect, but a visceral, emotional, joy-filled response born out of the wonder of God's loving and grace-filled nature towards all people.

Now I'm not in the least suggesting that there exists a theological straight line linking God's welcome of the non-Jew with the inclusion of those from the LGBT+ communities. But at that time, something did capture my heart about the nature of God and his love. As a Christian minister, I find it hard at times to differentiate between my personal faith and the public work that I do. Perhaps that is the point. God calls us to minister, not to compartmentalize private faith and public role, but precisely because he wants what he reveals to us in private to shape and define the teaching and leadership we share.

I have often said to congregations that at times it seems like they are paying me to explore my own faith and, in a sense, this is indeed what is happening. At one level, this obviously occurs as the minister sits in her or his study preparing the Sunday sermon. We are reading the text and are prayerfully open to the Holy Spirit and trusting that those things which God is revealing to us in the text are the very things which he wishes us to share with our churches. But why restrict that to preaching or teaching? Our modesty or self-effacing natures might demur from the idea that God uses our personal, subjective understanding to bless and build the church, and of course there are plenty of examples of how this might be abused through the insecure language of "God has told me that. . .." But I do believe that, rather incredibly and yet wonderfully, God has in his divine favor determined that, despite my flaws and limitations of character and intellect, I am useful for his purposes, and I must not baulk from this.

ADDRESSING OUR LIMITED WELCOME

So, we started to look at areas of the church where perhaps we were placing ungodly limitations on the welcome and inclusion of people in the life of the church family. Two very distinct areas emerged. The first regarded those with additional needs. Were we a church which did all we could to facilitate full participation of those with disabilities? We talked about this on Sundays, we discussed it in elders' meetings, and we spoke with those who had lived experience.

Whilst our building was fully compliant with all accessibility legislation, had a hearing loop and bright visuals, we saw holes in our assumed commitment to all. Learning new songs was hard for the visually impaired, so a monitor was set up in the congregation so that one member could have the words right in front of them, and large print Bibles were purchased for those who could be helped by them. We had some great Bible-readers in church, those especially gifted with delivery and diction. But one morning we invited someone new to read the passage. This church member had cerebral palsy and his diction was quite indistinct to those who didn't know him well and whose ear had not attuned to his way of speaking. But he mounted the platform, stood at the lectern, and brought us the church the reading for the day.

The second area of inclusion which we identified was that of ethnic minorities, or perhaps I should say, anyone who was not white. As a wealthy suburban church, ABC had for many years been monocultural, educated and middle class, and also mono-ethnic: a "white" church with few people from ethnic minorities. But somehow, things had changed over recent years and now almost a fifth of the congregation was non-white. Once again, we talked about this in church, changing who was profiled on Sunday mornings or who got to be on the platform. I read Malcolm Patten's excellent *Leading a Multi-Cultural Church*, which further developed my understanding and aided a shift in our practice with regards to hospitality, invitation, and participation. I knew that one significant change in this respect would be to have non-white elders. In all the church's 150-year history, I was unaware that there had ever been a black or Asian elder, and I spoke with the church and eldership about this. Despite unfortunate cries of tokenism from some members, I approached black members inviting them to become elders, but sadly they declined. It wasn't until the following year, 2020, that one accepted the invitation and was voted into the role a few months later.

Whilst the inclusion of those with additional needs and those from ethnic minorities should be uncontested and uncontroversial aspects of church life, there were two further matters which did challenge the church and our understanding of inclusion.

The first of these was National Lottery funding. Even though there is no Bible verse which explicitly states "thou shalt not gamble," I do accept the general principle that gambling is not something which the church encourages. Although not a gambler myself (except, if we are counting it, my pension fund), I have in my early twenties gambled on a few odd occasions on horse racing when attending meetings as "corporate hospitality" as a part of my previous career as an investment dealer for a merchant bank in the City of London. I don't do the lottery; in fact, many years ago, knowing my views, a non-Christian husband of a church member thought that it would be amusing to buy me a lottery ticket for my birthday. It won! Ten pounds. And at the following Sunday's baptism service, I took the winning ticket and set light to it as an illustration of how we must deny ourselves and give complete devotion to Christ. (Please don't ask me what I might have done if I had won fifty grand.) I have previously looked at whether the church may accept lottery funding for practical, serving ministries, but when I invited a discussion about this in my early days at ABC, it was quickly and firmly closed down. But the issue re-emerged when the church was informed that the council funding, which had been granted during the pandemic to help respond to community needs and had been such a success, would possibly now include some money from the National Lottery. Not only were the services we ran dependent on this funding, but jobs were too. So, hastily and expediently, we wrote a paper explaining why we felt that for these activities we could accept lottery funding and, in the summer of 2021, the church overwhelmingly voted in favor.

As a Baptist church, we have something called "membership." For those unaware of the nature of Baptist church life and governance, Baptist churches are congregational. Ultimate authority in the church is not the preserve of a bishop outside the church (episcopal), or a committee within the church (presbyterian), but is determined by the members of the church themselves (congregational). So, having attended the church over a period and deciding that this is to be their spiritual home, people apply to become members. Their names are brought before the church meeting—an occasional, usually midweek gathering to oversee and determine the important aspects of church life—and are voted in, becoming members of the church.

Whilst intended to be a simple and straightforward administrative process, membership can, subtly and wrongly, become "weaponized," a means to "vet" people who wish to become members. In essence, all that is required to become a member is a positive answer to three questions:

a. *Do you profess Christian faith, believing that "Jesus is Lord"?*

b. *Are you happy to do things in a Baptist way?*

c. *Do you want to join this group of believers, here in this place?*

If the answer to all those questions is yes, then people should be welcomed into membership. But what can happen is that other, wider aspects of the person, their life, their background can get dragged into the decision—hence a vetting approach emerges. What if the person is divorced, unmarried, or estranged from their partner? What if they are still a bit "sweary" or rub people up the wrong way? What if they attend church irregularly, or haven't yet offered to serve on a team? What if they are not PLUs—people like us?

THE STAKES BEGIN TO RISE

Around this time, a long-standing attender of the church asked to become a member. Whilst a mother of three teenage boys, she was not actually married to her partner, the father of the boys.

Within our Baptist constitution, the document which determines each church's legal basis, there is a section entitled, "The responsibilities of a church member normally include. . .." Whilst containing lots of useful stuff like giving to the church and serving in the church, it contains a line which, whilst good in intent, is profoundly ambiguous. It states that a church member will "uphold Christian values." What those values are is not defined, nor does it acknowledge that my Christian values may differ from yours in terms of politics, financial goals, the culture of my home, giving, etc. But these words became the battleground for the discussions as to whether this person be invited into membership. Of course, this line comes under "*responsibilities* of a church member," but these were not a list of conditions to *become* a church member. The guidance on the Baptist Union website is very clear that vetting is not something which is part of the membership process, but equally that accountability is crucial once someone has become a church member. So, the gateway is broad, but the responsibilities are then serious.

A few members became agitated by this application and some "heavy words were lightly thrown," reminding me of the saying, "Why is it that Christians get most upset with people who sin in different ways to how they themselves sin?" Around this time, that same member who, in preparing to preach, had asked about the church's view on homosexuality, approached me with something of a wry grin on his face and said, "Sometimes, Ash, I think it's easier to enter the kingdom of God than it is to become a member of Altrincham Baptist Church."

One of the things which we found helpful at this time was the writing of Stuart Murray Williams in his book, *The Church After Christendom*. In the book, Williams identifies what he sees as a biblical model for a church's understanding of what it is and therefore how participation happens. It has the following six points, which I shared with the church in one of our occasional "Inside Story" church communications.

- It has a definite center, comprising non-negotiable core convictions, rooted in the story which has shaped the community—and ultimately in Jesus Christ.

- This center is the focal point, around which members of the community gather enthusiastically.

- Its core convictions shape the church and separate it from other communities in a plural and contested culture.

- The church expends its energy on maintaining the core rather than patrolling the boundaries.

- Confidence in its core convictions frees the church to be inclusive, hospitable, and open to others, who are welcome to explore the community.

- Those who "belong" are moving towards the center, however near or far away they currently are in terms of belief or behavior.

You can see how significant this was for us and how it might shape our understanding of what we should do in this situation. I stated that we would have "core convictions" and not an Old Testament-like list of 613 laws. It speaks of no longer "patrolling the boundaries," hence vetting people for membership. Church participation (membership for us) was much more about a direction of travel. Were we moving closer to Jesus and each other? And if this was the case, then a freedom to be open, welcoming, and hospitable would undoubtedly develop.

But what about truth and fidelity? How might we retain faithfulness and, some might say, holiness, if we failed to differentiate who could be members apart from Ash's three stated criteria? Would we be selling out? Were we dropping our guard? Might we be throwing out our orthodoxy with the bath-water of judgementalism? These rules and traditions which we knew so well might feel clunky and unfit for purpose, but they were familiar, and taking an alternative route seemed to fly in the face of the doctrines and practices I had known throughout my life.

In all of this, I found that I was having to revisit my theology, work through what I had known, testing and assessing it against the revelation of Ephesians 3 and situations we were facing. If I could no longer apply Scripture in the blunt way I had done, how was challenge and change going to happen?

This would in no way be a free-for-all. The more inclusive church would still require such core convictions. However, I estimated that the change would be that, rather than using membership to "patrol the boundaries," we would be more trusting of the Holy Spirit to do his work in all our lives (1 Cor 2:4), trusting the Bible more, its core convictions guiding and shaping us (Heb 4:12), and trusting the redeeming power of God's people more—the community of believers faithfully living out the Christian life (Acts 2:43–47). These three—the Holy Spirit, the Bible and the redeeming Christian community—would have a renewed power and influence to take us on that journey of more Christ-like lives and draw others to become his disciples. This was the community I so wanted ABC to grow into and, so it seemed, did most of the church as well. When the meeting was held in the summer of 2022, once again the church acted for inclusion and voted overwhelmingly to welcome this new member.

TRUTH IN EVERY SITUATION

As an undergraduate at Spurgeon's College back in the early 1990s, I studied on the Church Planting and Evangelism track, as opposed to the Pastoral Ministry track. As a result, my dissertation had a distinctly missional theme: it was titled "The Gospel as Public Truth" and was based on the work of Bishop Lesslie Newbigin, a URC minister and missionary who, on his return from many years' service in India, was shocked to discover the degree to which Christian faith and influence had retreated from the public domain. This grabbed me. Having previously worked in a City of London dealing room and having tried to be a witness to my colleagues and the wider dealing community, I was strongly of the belief that my faith needed to be visible, engaged, open. As such, I developed a little mantra which went, "If this Christianity thing is actually true, then it must be true for everything. It must be true for economic policy, for how I parent my kids, for who I invite to my home." Please forgive me for my apparent flippancy, but I am deadly serious about this. I can't do with a half-hidden, half-hearted faith. It must have the confidence to engage with and address each and every matter.

So it was that we undertook a Sunday evening series on relatively controversial subjects. We looked at assisted suicide and then the question of transgendering. I specifically chose this because I had come to know another local minister, Steve Taylor, from South Manchester Community Church. Steve was an intelligent and erudite man with an easy manner and winning smile. He was a minister for just half the working week, because for the other half he was a GP working in practice. This gave Steve the wonderful advantage of not just talking about matters of medical science and ethics at church, but working them out during the week. Or was it the other way round? Did Steve's experience in the consulting room enrich and develop the understanding he shared on a Sunday morning? Steve had told me that he had done some work on transgender so, dodging the bullet, I invited him to speak one Sunday evening.

It was a good and interesting evening. Steve spoke freely and without notes, weaving together the Bible and his professional experience to ensure that almost no awkward or inconvenient aspect of the subject was left unaddressed. At the end, he invited questions. A hand shot up and the questioner then asked a question which perhaps we all wanted to ask but were too polite to do so: "Thanks for what you said, Steve, but. . ." (there had to be a but) ". . . you didn't say whether transgendering was a sin or not?" It was one of those Luke 4:20 moments, Jesus in Nazareth rolling up the scroll: "The eyes of all in the synagogue were fixed on him." Steve thought for a moment and replied, "My understanding of sin is that sin is rebellion against God." Good and orthodox so far. "So," he continued, "if in transgendering you are rebelling against God, then that is sinful. But if, however, in transgendering you are not rebelling against God, then I don't think that is sinful." A brilliant answer, and one which began to tease open questions about gender identity which would have further implications for the church.

2

The Tipping Point

THE LANDSCAPE OF THE CHURCH

HAVING WORKED TOGETHER AS an eldership team and church family on questions of greater inclusion and participation for those with additional needs and from ethnic minorities, it felt that somehow the landscape had opened up in such a way that we should now look at LGBT+ inclusion.

I had no prepared agenda to which I was working (as much as I was about to be accused of this by some), save that we were moving away from being a status quo, non-boat-rocking church. Our willingness to address challenging contemporary issues, and working through the pastoral realities of membership had in some way delivered us to a place where we might have the *ultimate* conversation. Ultimate, because it seemed clear that the question of LGBT+ inclusion was fast becoming the ground on which different factions of the church were drawing battle-lines, and this issue had become the litmus test of evangelical orthodoxy. The URC (2016) and Methodist (2021) denominations had already changed their official line on this matter, but as Baptists, we were part of what had historically been an overwhelmingly evangelical church and, as much as evangelical orthodoxy in the UK was shifting away from decrying homosexual orientation as being itself sinful to the belief that *only* homosexual practice was sinful, nationally it appeared that this was ground that would not be ceded without an almighty struggle.

PASTORAL MATTERS

The eradication of discrimination against same-sex-attracted people from a full welcome and participation in contemporary life, the workplace, or indeed as depicted on our TV screens, has come a long way from the culture of the 1970s. And yet within ABC, there existed members and families for whom having a gay sister, brother, daughter, son, grandchild, niece, or nephew was still a cause of embarrassment and shame. I knew this because people told me so. Over the previous few years, and perhaps because people had got to know and trust me as their minister, numbers of people had begun to share with me in private their own stories of having gay family members. Within these conversations, they also shared the hurt of what had happened when they had told this to Christian friends in church, or of the fear of what might happen if they did.

Two situations struck me most deeply. One couple shared the story of their son who met and married another man and had a child. The delight they might have had in sharing news of becoming grandparents, showing photos of their grandchild to friends in the church was, they felt, denied them because of how badly it had been received by those they had told that their son was gay. And then a mother, who explained that whilst having a gay son she still felt able to attend church and even attend after he was married to another man, went on to say, "Once he has a child with his husband, I don't feel that I could continue to come to church." These and other stories seemed justification enough for our need as a church family to talk about this.

NAMING THE ELEPHANT

Whilst I knew that we needed to talk, I was still quite unsure about what I thought on the matter. Yes, I was having conversations with other ministers and even around the family meal table with three daughters who were fully affirming and saw my view as outdated and anachronistic. But at the kitchen table I'd maintained the traditional view, consoling myself with the thought that Christian faith will at points contradict contemporary culture and this was just such an instance. But I was conflicted. Did we really *need* to talk about LGBT+ inclusion, or was this issue a bridge too far? Same-sex relations were traditionally taught as being sinful, so wasn't this the point at which we should love and welcome and yet deny acceptance and inclusion? I raised with the elders the question of whether we should consider, or perhaps reconsider, our views on the inclusion of same-sex-attracted people. We may decide not to change our view, but after considering it, we could at least hold that view with greater understanding.

I have always had great faith in the eldership teams I have worked with. They are the God-given, church-appointed group whose combined wisdom and responsibility is crucial in leading and guiding the church forward. They were a good bunch: women and men who were highly educated, worked in professional roles and who loved God and his church. But in those early conversations, there was caution and at points pushback from some to the idea of discussing LGBT+ inclusion. This seemed to stem from that sense that this was a non-question, one to which we already knew the answer, allied to it being the evangelical deal-breaker which we must pull back from.

To break the deadlock, one elder suggested that as the minister I should do a Bible study on the issue for the eldership team. Whilst appearing to be an appropriate and necessary step, I did sense that behind this suggestion there was the assumption that in doing a Bible study, the traditional evangelical view would undoubtedly prevail and we would thus be able to put this matter to bed once and for all.

I did the Bible study. It was September 2020, and we were still under lockdown conditions, so it happened online, admittedly hardly the best medium for undertaking such a subject. Some years previously I had done some work on the issue. I had taken the (unfortunately named) "clobber texts" and, using my commentaries, which were mostly published by IVP or similarly conservative publishers, I gave some understanding to these passages. I dug out this Bible study, dusted it down and developed some of the interpretations to fit the context to which I was speaking, i.e., elders considering the issue for the church. I spoke for about ninety minutes, a time interspersed with questions and comments.

I don't recall that any elder had ever previously undertaken a Bible study dedicated to this subject, therefore for each of us there seemed to be new understanding and nuances to what the passages and commentaries were teaching us. For some elders, this was revelatory. One elder commented on the fact that they were unaware that the Bible was silent on the matter of sexual orientation, only speaking about same-sex practice. But for others, the study was profoundly challenging. One reason for this was the conclusions I drew from the Old Testament passages, namely that they appeared to denounce inhospitality and homosexual rape, and not the matter which concerned us—that of consensual, loving, committed relationships of those in the LGBT+ communities. I had even cited a Baptist theologian who stated that, whilst they retained the traditional view, they found scant support for this in the pages of the Old Testament.

The elder who had first invited me to do the study grew increasingly irritated as the study reached its conclusion, and I and the other elders felt the rising tension. Far from ending discussion on the subject, the study had exposed some of the questions and uncertainties which surround LGBT+ inclusion. A week later, I contacted the agitated elder and invited them to go for a walk to talk through how they were feeling. We met and walked, doing laps of a local football field and, whilst it was somewhat helpful relationally to talk together, it did little to dampen the agitation they felt as they expressed their ire towards the subject and in part, by implication, towards me.

This was something I came to recognize with increasing clarity. From a number of people, I was getting the sense that, whilst there was both the subject and there was me as minister and those were two different things, they were slowly being melded together to become one. Disagreement with, and even dislike of, the subject could and would easily morph into antagonism and resentment towards me. This was set to become an aspect of the journey which would bring me the greatest personal cost over the next three years. The Bible study had been, in part, bruising, and so it seemed right to park the issue. However, it was to re-emerge in a surprising and dramatic way some five months later.

THE STRAW THAT BROKE . . .

Along with every church, we were living with the implications of the Covid-19 pandemic and the necessity to move our service online. The market value of the "techies" in church was high as they became the agents and facilitators of gathered church life. Music was pre-recorded, services became more managed and less spontaneous, and as a minister it seemed that I was having to learn the craft of a TV or radio presenter. At the start of the pandemic, I had contacted all those guests who were pre-booked to come a speak at ABC to cancel their engagements, as it only slowly dawned on me that I could of course "zoom in" just about anyone from anywhere across the globe, given the tech we now employed. But I have always been keen to use those within the church to speak and lead in services. These skills and gifts are not just the preserve of the trained and ordained, and so employing them from the church members brought richness and diversity to the diet of content, as well as being a blessing and encouragement to those who possessed these abilities and could use them.

I had for some time been keen to involve the young adults in church, a group whom I seemed to be wholly unsuccessful in persuading that attendance at church meetings, or becoming a member themselves, would be a good and positive step. I was therefore both surprised and delighted when one of my invitations to them was met with a positive response. I approached two young women in the church with the proposal that they preach together one Sunday morning. These were two women in their twenties, both able, educated, and impressive, but who both held some reservation about deeper involvement in ABC. My pitch to them was that they "tag-preached," sharing the sermon, with each giving two short inputs. They agreed. So, checking the preaching roster, I offered possible dates, and they settled on Sunday 21st February 2021, a date that now lives long in my memory.

I had planned a teaching series that would stretch from the New Year to Easter. It would be on the theme of "Leave the Ninety-Nine—Inspiring our Mission to the Lost." My intention was to help us to look beyond ourselves and focus on those outside of the church. In some sense, it was an obvious and simple idea, yet one which seemed not without controversy. As one member put it to me, without the slightest sense of irony, "It's all right looking for the lost one, but what about rest of us, the ninety-nine?"

The passage for 21st February was listed as Mark 5:25–34, looking at the double healing miracles of Jairus's daughter and the woman with the flow of blood, as it contained themes around including outsiders. Mark parallels the lives of these two women: one, the twelve-year-old daughter of the synagogue ruler who as such enjoyed a privileged status; the other, a woman whose twelve-year-long illness excluded her from the synagogue for being ritually unclean.

I like to think that I do a good job in resourcing and guiding those in the church who preach, providing all they need to do as well as they can. I have always ensured that I explain to them the wider themes of any series, give specific guidance about the passage and about the basics of preaching ("Stay tight to the text—that is where the power is!"), as well as photocopying Bible commentaries to aid their preparation. Given that this was the first sermon these two women would preach, I was determined that I would go above and beyond to equip them for the task.

The pandemic-provoked changes to Sundays had now become a familiar Sunday routine: clear the dining-room table, ensuring that the clutter of family life was hidden behind the screen; set up the laptop camera at the right height (an upturned orange B&Q bucket, I'd discovered, was just right to ensure it was at eye-level); log on fifteen minutes before the service to welcome people and have some valuable time of pastoral contact; watch as the tech team gave appropriate notice of the start time, then the countdown and finally start the service with a positive and bright welcome. On this particular Sunday, all seemed to go well. There were pre-recorded worship songs, various contributors in terms of engaging with families and the leading of prayers. And then, with some excitement, I announced that our message would be brought by two people new to preaching, handing over to the tech team to play their pre-recorded sermon. I sat back with anticipation.

The first of these young women started with confidence and eloquence. They explained the background to the passage, the context, and the general ideas it contained before handing over. The second preacher then developed the passage, what was going on in the story, explaining some of the subtleties and teasing out the meaning. As I was listening, I was thinking to myself, "This is good; this is really good." The first preacher returned and in her second stint began to nail the specific points, comparing and contrasting the two characters in the story and linking it all to our theme of leaving the ninety-nine. It was brilliant and I remember thinking that this was the best "first sermon" I had ever heard and doubtless everyone who was listening would be thinking just the same. Finally, she handed back to the second preacher who wrapped it all up. I can't now recall exactly her closing comments, but in her conclusion, she said very plainly that this passage was about inclusion and applied it thus: that for the church (ours and the wider church), the pressing issue of the day was the inclusion of LGBT+ people. Therefore, ABC should and indeed needed to include all LGBT+ people in the life of the church, welcoming them into membership, all areas of service and leadership responsibility. Amen.

The tech team switched to the final worship song, and I realized that I had three and a half minutes to try and say something which might. . . which might what? Ameliorate what they had said? Moderate it and give some caveat? Endorse it? At the very least, I didn't want to simply say something vacuous and crass, *something and nothing*. But that is exactly what I found myself doing. As the live stream switched back to me, I stumbled through something like, "Well, thank you to our preachers today for giving us some interesting and challenging thoughts. I'm sure it will have provoked lots of questions for further discussion. Now let's pray as we close the service."

We said our goodbyes over Zoom, and I turned off the computer, but somewhat more slowly and more thoughtfully than on previous occasions. I closed down the screen, pondering what might happen next. What happened was that my wife appeared at the dining-room door; she had been watching online in the front room. She looked across at me saying nothing. With faux positivity, I smiled and said, "What's up?" She said nothing, but instead walked over and stood by me, above me. I repeated the question, but this time with less confidence. Again, she didn't reply, but sat on my lap and began to cry. When she finally composed herself, for a third time I repeated, very gently, my question and this time she replied. She simply said, "I know what that is about to cost you."

THE REACTION

My phone began to ping and do so repeatedly. There were texts, WhatsApp messages and emails. Over the next twenty-four hours, I received thirty-two messages about the service, or more accurately the sermon, easily surpassing the highest number provoked by any sermon I or anyone had preached at ABC. Eleven of those messages were from people expressing how deeply troubled they were about what had been shared in the sermon. Admittedly, I was receiving people's initial, emotive reaction to the message, before they had perhaps had time to process what had been said and modify what they wrote. But these people were upset, some were angry and some "spitting feathers." The other twenty-one messages all spoke in favor of what they had heard. They said how well these two women had both spoken and they were glad that the issue had been raised. Some even, rather awkwardly for me, commended me for daring to raise the subject, which I obviously hadn't; indeed, it would have been cowardly on my part to have others bring this subject to the attention of the church. Some of the messages were from elders. "Brave!" was the most positive; others were circumspect and some deeply agitated.

I messaged both women, thanking them for the sermon and expressing how well they had done. I didn't want them to get any impression from me that I was unhappy with what they had done. I wasn't, and indeed, I knew my responsibility was to try and shield them from any criticism which was rightly mine. It was me who had invited them to speak, and me who had given them this text. Over the next forty-eight hours, I rang and spoke with each of the eleven people who had found the sermon unhelpful and disturbing. It was my responsibility. With most people, the conversations were calm and respectful. They wanted to know whether I had put them up to this and whether I had known what they were going to say—to both of which I could readily answer "No."

One conversation does, however, stick in my mind. I called one man, an older retired man whose wife answered the phone and, with an ominous tone, warned me about her husband's anger and upset before passing the phone to her husband. It's a comedy cliché to have to hold your phone away from your ear, so loud is the voice that is speaking to you, but that is exactly what I found myself doing in this call. He was furious. Furious with the women who spoke, furious that the subject had been talked about in this way and most of all, furious with me for allowing all this to happen. As the call continued, slowly he began to calm down, and I could bring the phone to my ear. He spoke of the inclusion of LGBT+ people as being "a woke agenda" and that the church was in danger of simply "aping the culture of the day." The conversation then took a surprising turn as he switched track, railing against the fact that we no longer sang many hymns in church and that we should, as hymns contained substance and meaning which modern songs lacked. He then told me that another problem with society was that every TV advertisement now included a black person—every one! All part of what he saw as the woke agenda which was taking over.

Surprising and shocking even, as some of these comments might appear, I was at least able to make some sense of what I was hearing. What I thought I was hearing was an older, retired man, a daily reader of his paper, who was keenly watching society and culture. And what he was seeing was that things were shifting rapidly before his eyes. So rapidly in fact, that he could no longer cope with the change and rate of change he was witnessing, and he wanted it to stop. And when this change entered the last bastion of all that was familiar, safe, and constant for him—his church— then he could no longer remain silent. This Sunday message had become the focus for all of that angst, all that disturbed him, and all that he disagreed with.

CONSEQUENCES

As a result of the sermon, one member resigned their membership the following day and joined a local Anglican church. Some others decided to start "attending" other churches online. After all, this was the time of the great "runaround," where it was easy to privately check out alternatives to the church you attended, given the medium of Zoom. If people had suspicions about Ashley and the direction of the church, given the decisions made over recent years and the openness to engage with difficult subjects, then this provided a tipping point to make a move to a more familiar and less challenging church experience. Over the next twelve months, many local churches would benefit numerically from the conversation we were about to have at ABC.

The next elders' meeting was also interesting. At first, it felt like interrogation. I had to explain how it was possible that such a message could be publicly stated without my knowledge or prior approval. My answer, that I didn't know what was going to be said, provoked the response by some that I *should* have known. I should have listened to the sermon before it was preached to "protect the pulpit." Perhaps I should have listened to it beforehand but, in my thirty years of ministry, I have never done this or felt the need to "protect the pulpit." If we are a mature congregation, then surely we are grown up enough to trust our preachers and, if necessary, review any content and subsequently challenge what has been said.

During my time at ABC, I had heard several church members preach on occasion with dubious interpretations or dodgy exegesis, but this didn't seem to be the appropriate moment to say this. I was being challenged by some elders to come down hard on what had been preached and issue a corrective statement, but I wanted to talk about this subject and, as much as this was quite unplanned, it was a reminder that the issue was not going to go away. I was also asked directly as to my own view on the matter. I demurred. I said that I thought it unhelpful to express my opinion as it would stymie open conversation and discussion, but even in not coming out with a view, I seemed to some to be saying something.

I asked the elders whether this might be the right time to open the conversation about LGBT+ inclusion. Whilst some thought it might be, other louder voices said no. We were still in a pandemic and there were different priorities at this time. Whilst I was keen to explore the issue, I did and do accept the decision (it's how Baptist churches work), even though there was the sense that we were simply kicking it down the road. The matter was deferred, albeit with a communication to the church that we would discuss it together in due course. Some were upset about any delay, because the issue affected them daily and waiting seemed unnecessary. Four months later, in June 2021, I again approached the elders with a request for a church-wide discussion. Again, it was deferred. I asked again in September, and they said yes.

3

Devising the Process

MAKING A PLAN

IT HAD BEEN EXACTLY a year since I had undertaken the Bible study with the elders and we were now ready, or as ready as we might ever be, to have a church-wide conversation about the nature of inclusion of those from LGBT+ communities in church life. The make-up of the eldership team had changed slightly, given that each July at the church's AGM some elders step down, having completed their term, and new elders are elected. Overall, the composition of the new eldership team seemed to be more open to the idea of a conversation than had previously been the case.

The agreement to talk about the subject did have a condition and a caveat. The condition was that it was me who had to come up with a comprehensive plan for how we might have "the conversation," and the caveat was that the elders retained the power to veto the plan I made, which I guess only seemed fair and right.

This was the point then at which the rubber hit the road. We were about to enter a realm which is deeply contested and emotive, a place indeed where angels might fear to tread. The stakes were high for me, but I have always believed that I as a minister am eminently dispensable. Just as a bicycle has a sacrificial "hanger" designed to break in the event of a crash to ensure that a more valuable derailleur component is preserved, I consider that I am not actually so important. The most important matter was the family of the church, and the Bible tells us that any misleading of the church is subject to millstones around necks. James chapter 3 also explains that I, as a teacher in the church, would be judged even more severely. These factors certainly relativize any undue focus on self.

As any church leader will tell you, there is a sense that, just as in education, September heralds the start of a new year. Here was a new opportunity for the church. However, the period from September through to Christmas is habitually the busiest time in the church's calendar. There are new initiatives, activities around Harvest, and then the planning for Advent. Christmas always requires significant preparation, creativity, and work as the church celebrates the incarnation, and takes the opportunity to share this wonderful news with its wider community. As such, it seemed that to add the additional component of a conversation about LGBT+ inclusion would all be too much; we would wait until the New Year.

As a minister rubbing shoulders with other church leaders, you get to find out what is going on in wider church life, and so I was hearing how a few other churches had looked at this question, either formally through a process or by dipping their toe in. I had heard that some had arrived at a new understanding, changing their practice to welcome LGBT+ people into their churches. I also heard how the question had been raised in churches where things had not gone that way, and initial attempts to consider the issue had quickly led to the matter being closed down, with attendant tension and antagonism. Some other churches simply determined to maintain the traditional view. I was attentive to what was happening around me and was trying to sift what I heard—the wheat of the good and the chaff of the unhelpful—and all of this with a mind on ABC, where were we at and what would be helpful here.

WHAT MIGHT THE PROCESS LOOK LIKE?

In my mind, there were some obvious features which would be necessary for the process. We would look at the Bible and attempt as much as we could to be Spirit-led, and objectively and fair-mindedly allow the Bible to speak to us. We would have to have times of open and hopefully respectful discussion and conversation. We would need to provide additional material—pointing people to websites or books which would help the process. I also thought that we were likely to invite those from outside the church to bring some input, probably one from either side of the debate, to help us appreciate the view which we didn't instinctively own ourselves. And we would have to listen. Listen to each other and to God; we would commit to prayer.

Here again were my three enablers of Christian enlightenment and transformation at work in this one defined subject: the Bible, the Holy Spirit and the Christian community all combining to bring about . . . well, we would see what the conclusion would be.

CREATING SANCTUARY

At this time, I had become aware of a course which had recently been established to help churches consider LGBT+ inclusion. *Creating Sanctuary*[1] was devised by a mostly Baptist-led group with one sole stated aim. In the light of the tragic death of teenager Lizzie Lowe, who took her own life believing that her sexual orientation was at odds with the Christian life, the course was established to help prevent such a tragedy being repeated. Its stated aim is:

> *Where people are in a minority, excluded, vulnerable or at risk, we have a shared moral and ethical responsibility to safeguard against doing more harm. Our churches should be a safe place for everyone.*[2]

1. https://www.creatingsanctuary.org.uk/
2. https://www.creatingsanctuary.org.uk/introduction

Practically, the course was five weeks long and would be led by facilitators from the *Creating Sanctuary* team, a team which included several significant figures from national Baptist life. We could run the course through Zoom, so accessibility for the church would not be a problem. And the content looked good. The weekly sessions would cover the following ground:

1. Understanding the lived experience of the LGBT+ community in our churches and faith communities.

2. Relating the stories of the LGBT+ community to our own lived experience and specifically to the people we know or love who are within our community.

3. A discussion of faith sector leaders and reflection on the biblical principles of inclusion.

4. Exploring the hallmarks of a healthy and safe culture.

5. Listening to, and learning from, the experiences of other churches who have journeyed together to become welcoming or affirming.

One particularly attractive aspect for me of running *Creating Sanctuary* was that I was not having to provide the content, nor was I the focus of the conversation. Here was an outside group, who were bringing their input and were looking at one clear and hopefully uncontested aspect of the inclusion question. Could we at least agree that we didn't want ABC to be a church where the tragedy of this young girl's suicide would be repeated?

LITERATURE

Whilst research supports the view that Christians are less inclined to read their Bibles than they once were, it is also the case that we have access to more information than ever before. We are constantly reading and absorbing information through the news, advertisements, and social media. Each of these impact us in some way. There is a mass of Christian literature on the issue of homosexuality whether books, articles, or the bite-sized Tweet.

Having read extensively on the issue, I had found that many books had titles which rather over-confidently tethered the Bible to their stated position. *Jesus the Bible and Homosexuality*[3], *What Does the Bible Teach about Homosexuality?*[4] *The Bible on the Question of Homosexuality*[5]. *What does the Bible Really Teach About Homosexuality?*[6] *What the Bible Really Says About Homosexuality.*[7] And the claim of those last two books to have the "real" truth seems somewhat oxymoronic (the author doth protest too much, methinks.) What we needed was a book, or books, which were less dogmatic and more fair-minded about this contested issue. Perhaps an author might even be willing to acknowledge strengths in the arguments of those owning a different view, and possibly even the weaknesses in their own position.

I landed on two books which I thought might get us closer to such an approach. Ed Shaw's *The Plausibility Problem*[8] is written by a same-sex-attracted Anglican minister and is disarming in the way in which he honestly shares his struggles as a gay man who nonetheless chooses to retain celibacy, as he believes that this is the life, the best life, which God calls him to. The other book was David Gushee's *Changing Our Mind.*[9] Gushee, a leading ethicist from the United States, was once an advocate of the traditional view, having set out his reasons in a work which had become the standard textbook for Christian ethics in American theological colleges. However, as the title suggests, he changed his mind, and this book sets out in a plain and accessible way how and why he changed his view.

3. Rogers, *Jesus the Bible and Homosexuality*
4. Peacock, Strachan, *What Does the Bible Teach about Homosexuality*
5. Himbaza, Schenker et al., *The Bible on the Question of Homosexuality*
6. DeYoung, *What does the Bible Really Teach About Homosexuality?*
7. Helminiak, *What the Bible Really Says About Homosexuality*
8. Shaw, *The Plausibility Problem*
9. Gushee, *Changing Our Mind*

During the process, another book came to our attention which we also found extremely helpful. *Two Views on Homosexuality, the Bible, and the Church*[10] is a book with four authors. Two hold the traditional view, and two the affirming position. In the book, each presents their rationale for the position they hold, but here's the kicker. After each essay the other three comment on and critique what the essayist has written, all within a highly respectful framework. Not only is the content helpful, but here we found a model for how different views can effectively speak, listen, understand, and respond to each other—perhaps the "holy grail" of a discernment process.

VERSION 1.0

So that autumn, I told the church that we would start a conversation in the New Year, and later announced the exact form the process would take. The first stage would involve undertaking five weeks of the *Creating Sanctuary* course, and we directed people to the website, inviting them to read up on it before we began. The second stage would be a process of learning, listening, discussing, and discerning our view on the inclusion of LGBT+ people in the life of the church. This would include careful examination of the Bible, considering our theology, listening to testimony and, vitally, praying together. In this, we would invite a range of input leading to ABC's considered discernment on this important issue.

I wince as I look back on this now. Yes, it was the best I could come up with at the time but, looking back, it also seems a little thin on detail. Who would give the input, share testimony, shape the content? When would this happen, in what forms, and how accessible would it be? When would it end? And what was the endgame? What ultimately would be the question on which the church would be deciding?

Whilst my personality type is inherently "blue-sky," an obvious frustration to those who like things more detailed and

10. Loader, DeFranza, et al., *Two Views on Homosexuality, the Bible, and the Church*

clear-cut, I sensed that the process was something which would evolve. I was clear about the fact that I simply didn't know where the church would be after we had completed *Creating Sanctuary*. Would this be the *amuse bouche* which left people eagerly wanting to dive into the main course, or would it leave a bad taste in the mouth, meaning that we had little appetite for going on? There is a time and a place for planning, and there is equally a time for making things up as we go along. The level of uncertainty with the process and how people might respond at each stage meant that I was strongly drawn to a more intuitive approach.

ELDERSHIP TENSIONS

As I have already explained, the eldership at the time had unanimously agreed to start this process and overall had expressed a greater openness to exploring the issue than had previously been the case. In deciding this, they were taking a bold step. It should not be glossed over that while the burden of church leadership was for me, a minister, part and parcel of my role, it was not so straightforward for those church members who have offered time, energy, mental and, at times, emotional resources to poke their heads above the parapet of church life and serve in a leadership role. One Vineyard Church minister would cite John Wimber, who apparently said, "Becoming a leader is like volunteering to be ugly." Confidence and trust in me by the elders were going to be exercised through this process. I needed to be aware of this and ensure that I knew how each of them was feeling. Maintaining, as best I could, healthy and open relations with each elder would be vital, something which I was later to find would be stretched to breaking-point.

Coincidentally, the eldership team had, some six months earlier, undertaken a course with other church leadership teams aimed at exploring how we discerned together. The brainchild of Baptist minister Simon Hall, Northern Baptist College's Edifi training had run a course aimed at helping leadership teams explore the process of corporate discernment. The coursebook which accompanied the training was Ruth Haley Barton's brilliant *Pursuing God's Will Together: A Discernment Practice for Leadership Groups*[11]. There were two key teachings from this course which had practical benefits for us as elders. The first concerned our need for *indifference*. Whilst indifference is usually viewed in pejorative terms, Haley Barton suggests that indifference is an essential aspect of church leadership.

> "The first and most essential dynamic of discernment is the movement towards indifference. . . In the context of spiritual discernment, indifference is a positive term signifying that 'I am indifferent to anything but God's will.'"[12]

The second key point was the move away from a binary Yes/No response to making decisions. Instead, Haley Barton proposed that there might be four possible responses to a matter, especially a matter that was complicated and involved. In summary she suggests the following four options*

1. Yes, I wholeheartedly agree with the proposal and am happy to support it.

2. Whilst I have some reservations, on balance I think there are more positives, so will support the proposal.

3. I have reservations and am not personally convinced. But, looking around the room I can see that I am in the minority. I trust my team's wisdom and respect their views, so although I don't agree I will not stand in the way of the majority.

4. No, I disagree with the proposal and cannot support it. So, I ask that we do not agree this and go back to finding another way.

Not only does this move us away from the limitations of polarized responses, it also recognizes and acknowledges that we will not always make decisions with 100 percent certainty, but often with some reservation. It also accepts the fact that "one mind" need not necessarily mean unanimity. As a team we might make a decision,

11. Haley Barton, *Pursuing God's Will Together*
12 Haley Barton, *Pursuing God's Will Together*, 63–64 & 219

but this "one mind" may indeed be made up of different views. This would be valuable, as we would later discover.

One of the manifestations of a desire to make ABC more inclusive had been to end the white hegemony which had held sway in the church. Over a couple of years, I had encouraged the church to consider and recommend non-white elders. Whilst this had not been followed through with an appointment in 2020, it did happen in 2021, with the appointment of our first black elder. He was an intelligent, engaging, and earnest family man of west African heritage, and we were blessed to have him as a part of the team. He was also a keen student of the Bible and of theology and, during the autumn of 2021, we would occasionally meet for lunchtime walks where we would discuss theology and biblical interpretation. In those conversations, he also expressed something of his hesitancy and reticence towards the idea of the upcoming discussion on LGBT+ inclusion, a hesitancy that he expressed in terms of his belief that same-sex orientation, let alone activity, was sinful and opposed to God's will.

As a part of our preparation for the start of discussions in the New Year, we had planned an elders' overnight stay on the Welsh border. Within the program I had invited a gay Baptist minister to share the story of his life and reflect on this in terms of his Christian faith. He would arrive on Saturday morning with the intention of sharing his story of faith *and* same-sex attraction. It was our opportunity as elders to hear personal testimony together in a way which we were unlikely to have done before.

On the Friday night, we all began to gather for our overnight stay, arriving in dribs and drabs, but one of our number was missing. Our newly appointed elder was nowhere to be seen, and we were approaching the time when we would start our first session. I checked my phone, but there were no messages, so I rang him. He answered and I asked where he was and whether he was okay. His reply, I could sense, was given with a heavy heart. He explained that he had been wrestling with whether he should attend and had concluded that he shouldn't come. His reason was to do with the fact that meeting with a gay minister was simply too challenging for him and regretfully he would not be coming. This obviously placed something of a cloud over our time away, and I was saddened to receive a few days later a letter from him explaining in the most careful and respectful terms that after prayer and further consideration, he would be resigning from the eldership and from the church, as he believed that his position was incompatible with what he saw as the direction of travel that ABC was taking. We spoke together and I expressed my regret at this news, thanking him and his family for their involvement and service in the life of ABC.

However, on the Saturday morning, we had the privilege of hearing a painfully honest and significant testimony of how someone from the queer community and of charismatic faith had initially sought to be delivered from his sexual orientation, before rejecting church and Christian faith and then finally finding a place of peace, both with his own queerness and the faith he could not deny. This was important for all of us present, delivering us from assumptions and misunderstanding, and modelling how a deep and costly faith might indeed be held hand-in-hand with same-sex orientation. This shifted us from the ignorance of theory to the pastoral reality of what this means in the lives of individuals.

This was early December 2021, and we hadn't yet started any formal process. We had already received one member's resignation and some were drifting away from the church and looking at other churches. But the elder who resigned was the first to express to me that they believed the church to be on a course with a definite destination. Perhaps I was naïve in thinking that we weren't, that we were simply looking at a subject and attempting to listen afresh to what God would say to us. But that is what I was repeatedly telling myself. As I reflected on and evaluated my intentions and motivations, I returned to the same conclusion, namely that we needed to look at this issue and indeed be indifferent to any conclusion apart from that to which God would lead us.

4

Starting the Process

CREATING SANCTUARY

7.30PM, TUESDAY 22ND FEBRUARY 2022: the first session of *Creating Sanctuary*. Although I was hopeful of a good attendance, I was surprised that more than a hundred people logged on to the first session. In total, around 120 would attend at least some of the course and each week there were not less than ninety present. However, I immediately spotted a problem.

Because of previous conversations or emails, I did have a reasonable idea of what some in the congregation thought about the issue, particularly those who stood at either end of the spectrum. As I flicked through the Zoom screens, the problem I observed was that whilst I could see some of those who had expressed a traditional view, there were many more who held this view who were not present. I was disappointed. Perhaps the reason for this was like that given by one elder who had asked not to be a discussion group facilitator, a role I had invited the elders to take, explaining that he felt that in some way his participation would suggest his tacit approval to an affirming view. Over the coming weeks, I was to discover that in fact he had decided not to attend any of the

35

course. Once again, that gnarly problem arose of how to discuss something which some people didn't want to discuss. How could we look at this issue together when some of our church family would absent themselves? It may have been naïve of me to expect that all with a keen interest or concern about the matter would attend, but it would have been equally naïve to think that there were no other forums, conversations, or discussions springing up away from the shared space of church-wide gatherings.

I welcomed the attenders and our two facilitators. Luke Dowding is a Baptist deacon, holds degrees in theology and biblical studies, and is Executive Director for OneBodyOneFaith, the first Christian LGBT+ members' network to be formed in the UK. Myra Blyth is a Baptist minister, former Deputy General Secretary of the Baptist Union, and previously worked for the World Council of Churches: Inter-Church Aid and The Refugee World Service. I prayed before handing over the evening to Luke. Luke's calm, deliberate and non-judgmental manner set the tone well. He also began, as he would each week, by reading through the ground rules for the course.[1] There were nine and they covered guidance

1. https://www.creatingsanctuary.org.uk/ground-rules
Lesbian, Gay, Bisexual and Transgender siblings in the room have the least systematic privilege and power and are at risk of harm in church settings. Their voices will be given additional respect, their experiences will be treated with respect, care and met with love.
   a. We will listen carefully to each other, with respect, allowing all views to be heard, without interruption and consciously not speaking or behaving in a way that causes further harm to LGBT+ siblings.
   b. We will seek to be genuine and honest.
   c. What we say in this room is confidential, details are not for sharing without agreement.
   d. We will be respectful and polite. We will exercise grace and restraint.
   e. We will be careful with our language and recognise that we will sometimes hurt each other without meaning to. Your intention is not always your impact; we will recognise impact together.
   f. If in doubt, respectfully ask for clarification.
   g. If something challenges you, embrace the challenge and try and learn from it.
   h. If you feel unsafe or distressed at any time, it is important to leave the room; we will make sure someone is on hand to talk about what's happened and how you're feeling.
   i. We will maintain confidentiality. We will not discuss information about

which addressed both our thinking and internal attitude, as well as the way in which we expressed ourselves publicly. These would prove to be an important aspect of the course, as their weekly repeating meant that at no point was it evident that the discussions in breakout rooms were anything other than respectful and gracious. In fact, I was immensely proud of the way in which everyone conducted themselves in each public forum throughout the whole discernment.

The course went well. It was gentle and non-dogmatic. It included a range of inputs, and the contributions from those with lived experience seemed especially valuable in dispelling myths and assumptions. And of course, there were discussions in breakout rooms. Nobody had to contribute, and no record was being kept of who said what, enabling a good degree of openness and honesty. It wasn't, of course, without its detractors. Some expressed their view that the style of presentation verged on the sanctimonious. Some said, and were perhaps justified in saying, that the content was presented by those who were all supportive of an affirming view. But after all, the course had one stated aim: helping churches to be places where those from LGBT+ communities would only be met with kindness and love.

Numbers remained strong throughout the course, and the five weeks seemed to go very quickly. Surprisingly perhaps, I was not assailed by questioning emails or those "Could I have a word with you?" conversations on Sunday mornings. In essence, the course did what I had hoped it would do. Despite the absences I previously referred to, it had opened the subject of LGBT+ inclusion in a non-controversial and apparently helpful way. It showed that this was a subject which we could talk about and gave us confidence to press on. But press on with what?

---

other people without their informed consent. What we discuss together today remains confidential.

37

AUTHORITY AND THE BIBLE

The one topic which everyone now wanted to look at was the Bible. As evangelicals, the Bible is and remains the place we go to for truth. Of course, on this matter there is a subtle, yet important, difference between the World Evangelical Alliance's statement of faith and the Baptist Union Declaration of Principle. The World Evangelical Alliance statement explains:

> We believe in: The Holy Scriptures as originally given by God, divinely inspired, infallible, entirely trustworthy; and the supreme authority in all matters of faith and conduct.[2]

The Baptist Union's Declaration states:

> That our Lord and Saviour Jesus Christ, God manifest in the flesh, is the sole and absolute authority in all matters pertaining to faith and practice, as revealed in the Holy Scriptures.[3]

It is a person, not a book, who is our ultimate authority, albeit that what we know of the person is primarily found in the Bible. It was now late March, and Easter was fast approaching. Time to take our foot off the gas and switch our attention to activity around Holy Week.

I describe the plan I shared with the elders to discuss LGBT+ inclusion as version 1.0. That was because I was more inclined to make things up as we went along to respond to what was happening and where the church was after each stage. Do we need to slow down and revisit something? Do we need to pause and allow people to cool off? Was the subject all too challenging and this was proving to be the wrong time—so perhaps we should stop? We had a plan, but a plan that could be amended. This afforded us the opportunity to respond and adapt it whenever it was appropriate.

Over the Easter period, there were two decisions that I came to. The first was that it was indeed the right time for us to turn to the Bible. The second was perhaps more difficult and yet had

---

2. World Evangelical Alliance, *Statement of Faith*, lines 2–3
3. Baptists Together, *Declaration of Principle*, lines 2–4

become more obvious. Rather than invite someone from outside the church to talk about the Bible and LGBT+ inclusion, or indeed invite those with different views on the Bible to share differing perspectives, I decided that I would undertake these studies myself. Whilst I was very clear that I wanted to be fair to all through this process, not expressing bias, the idea of farming out responsibility for searching the scriptures seemed plain wrong. I was the one who was ultimately responsible for shaping the church's theology and understanding. I was the one who most Sundays would teach the Bible. To not take this on myself felt like an abrogation of duty.

Crucial to this was also the idea that what we were doing was Christian discernment as a faith community. This was not a courtroom where evidence was being presented for and against, with the implication that in some way the members represented the jury who would decide the matter on a majority basis. Neither was this arbitration. We were not looking to arrive at some middle consensus position where all parties would be appeased, despite the possibility that the conclusion would be vague and accommodating. Nor was this mediation, simply designed to maintain relationships above all things. No, we were looking to discern together, one view as a whole church, or as much as a whole church as we could possibly be.

The BU Declaration of Principle I cited earlier in fact goes on to say the following, ". . . and that each Church has liberty, under the guidance of the Holy Spirit, to interpret and administer His laws." That was what we were doing: looking to Jesus, our ultimate authority, as revealed in the scriptures and, under the guidance of the Holy Spirit, seeking to interpret and administer his laws together.

I set two dates in May for the church to gather, this time in person, to look at LGBT+ inclusion, considering what the Bible does and doesn't teach, and set about preparing for them. Having led the eldership's Bible study, I already had much of the material I would use. But given my constant reading on the subject, my thinking and praying for clarity and my endless conversations with people, my own understanding was shifting. Indeed, just as with

Locard's basic principle of forensic science, where "every contact leaves a trace," all these engagements were developing in me a new and more informed view.

BIBLE STUDIES

We held the two studies on the 17th and 24th May, and around 75 people attended each week, with only those unable to attend through work, age, or illness able to access online. I wanted everyone who was able to be in the room. There was something important about being present in the same space, being with other people, watching as well as listening, fully engaging in what was happening. In essence, the content was simple: week one—the Old Testament; week two—the New Testament; begin each week with testimony.

On the first week, this meant having a married couple together and then on the second a mother, briefly sharing the story of their experience of having a gay child and how this had affected their faith and their relationships in the church. These were both listened to attentively, with the members expressing their gratitude to them at the end. I was most grateful to them for their willingness to share their stories. I would then cite the ground rules we had learned from *Creating Sanctuary*, before moving to the main part of our time together. I would identify and analyze key verses or passages which were salient to the issue and, using an array of commentaries and other books, present different interpretations (essentially the traditional and the affirming view) on each of the passages. I would give out full notes to all who attended and later emailed them to all on the church contact list.

After examining each passage, I would then explain as a brief postscript the view I had of that passage. This became the first time I would publicly state how I interpreted these verses, something I had previously been reticent to do, even though some had repeatedly pressed me to do this ever since the study with the elders.

I would also speak for most of the ninety minutes each study took. This was not because I wanted to limit the time of discussion, but simply because we had a lot of ground to cover. As a minister, I'm often trying to balance the need to be full and comprehensive in what I say with a brevity which keeps people engaged, interested and awake! I therefore repeated my oft-cited mantra of "Please call me, email me, message me at any point in the coming weeks with views, opinions or questions you may have about what I share."

I've already stated that the purpose of this book is not to look at the theology or undertake a Bible study of the subject. This book is about people and leadership, a church undertaking an exercise in discernment. But there were some aspects to these weeks which seem worthy of note. There is no set "canon" of texts to study. Yes, there are those verses which now seem to bear the unfortunate title of "clobber texts," so-called because these have historically been the verses that some with the traditional view have used (in the eyes of those of the affirming view) to "clobber" those in the LGBT+ community. I looked at all those passages, namely Genesis 19, Judges 19, Leviticus 18 and 20, and then the three Pauline passages of Romans 1, First Corinthians 6 and First Timothy 1.

There were, though, other passages I believed to be important in helping our discernment. For example, Genesis 1 and 2, for all that it said about gender and relationships between male and female, and for all that it didn't say about celibacy, the inability or unwillingness to have children, the lack of a suitable partner, or a sex-less marriage, etc.

We also looked at some passages from the Gospels. Whilst in specific terms the four Gospels seem to be silent on the matter of same-sex relations, these books do contain teaching about sexual sin, eunuchs and how we are to interpret the law—all of which had some bearing on our discernment.

Finally, the account of Peter's revelation about God's inclusion of Gentiles, detailed in Acts 10, provided a significant framework for appreciating how our understanding of a theological issue might change.

Some of the content of those studies was complicated for the average church member. When you start referring to the original Greek language and specific words that appear in the Pauline texts—*malakoi* or *arsenokoitai*—whilst you are being diligent in your research, you also must acknowledge that for some this can be difficult to understand.

There are also wider theological issues to reflect on. This essentially includes the approach you choose to take with regards to assessing the relevance or otherwise of some of the 613 Old Testament laws in the contemporary age. I determined that there were three main approaches.

Firstly, there is the Reformed view. This is the preferred method of the Reformers and Reformed church and was devised by Thomas Aquinas (1225–1274). It takes the laws of the Old Covenant and sets them in three categories: moral, civil, and ceremonial laws. It concludes that ". . . only the moral laws of the Mosaic Law, which include the Ten Commandments and the commands repeated in the New Testament, directly apply to Christians."[4]

Secondly, there is Principlism. The claim of Principlism is that it ". . . seeks to find universal principles in the Old Testament citation legal material and to apply these principles to believers today." This approach is more consistent than the traditional one, and it is more reflective of sound hermeneutical method. It also allows believers to see that all Scripture is "useful for teaching, rebuking, correcting and training in righteousness."[5]

Finally, there is the approach of New Covenant Theology. This third approach states that the Law is applicable only when renewed in the New Testament. For example, Jesus said that he had not come to abolish the Law, but to fulfil it (Matt 5:17–18), but he also said that he was bringing a new covenant (Luke 22:19–20) based on a new law, the law of love (John 13:34). With this in mind, it is concluded that the commands of the Old Testament are not binding on Christians, except where they are specifically renewed under the New Covenant. For example, the Ten Commandments are each expressed and affirmed in the New Testament. We

4. www.wikipedia.org/wiki/Christian_views_on_the_Old_Covenant (See also, www.christian.org.uk/wp-content/uploads/the-threefold-division-of-the-law.pdf)

5. 2 Tim 3:16

assessed the merits of each and invited the members to determine their own approach.

The bulk of the commentaries I was using were from publishers who have traditionally been associated with a conservative evangelical position. They were books published by IVP, John Knox, or NIV commentaries, but I also quoted material from books by both conservatives (Kevin de Young, John Kohlenberger III, Stanley Grenz, etc.) and progressives (David Gushee, John Zehring and William Loader, etc.).

ACKNOWLEDGING BIAS

At the start of week one, I shared with the church a template of options which exist regarding people's views. I wanted to help people think about the position they held in advance of the studies we were about to have. Afterwards we could then assess any potential change brought about by the studies. I also felt it important to explain to the church that I was biased in my views. In fact, what I said was, "I've heard from several people that supporting the idea of LGBT+ inclusion is just a woke agenda. It's younger people and younger adults in the church simply aping the culture of the day. That may or may not be the case; I haven't spoken to everyone who holds an affirming view so can't make that judgement. But the judgement I can make is that by being born in 1965 I too was molded and shaped by the culture I grew up in. My understanding and outlook were influenced by what I saw on television and observed around me. What I had observed was that it was normal for white people to paint their faces black and sing about the 'Camptown Races' in the name of Saturday night entertainment. And on how homosexuality was portrayed, I loved watching the BBC comedies *It Ain't Half Hot Mum*, which included actor Melvin Hughes playing Bombardier 'Gloria' Beaumont, John Inman playing the effeminate Mr. Humphries in *Are You Being Served?*, or even Larry Grayson's camp hosting of *The Generation Game*. I laughed along with the rest of them. I am biased, and perhaps the younger adults are biased. But don't let us think that any of us are a cultural blank page where our judgement has remained untainted by the things we have imbibed over the decades. That is simply not the case."

There is one further observation about bias I'd want to identify. This is to do with the assumed starting- point for the discernment process. As an evangelical church exploring this issue, we come to it not with no view, but usually from an inherited and assumed position. For most evangelicals (although as my previous experience demonstrates, not for all), the view remains that whilst homosexual orientation is not in and of itself sinful, homosexual activity is sinful and against the Bible's teaching. It was backed up by an historic interpretation of Scripture and the teaching of the church over two millennia, let alone the cultural antipathy which had only in recent years been reversed. I reflected that in my own whole-life experience of fifty-seven years in the church, I had very rarely heard a sermon, or attended a study where the theme of same-sex practice was the sole subject, and had only twice spoken on the subject myself. My, and the church's, understanding was, it seemed, a product of occasional references in sermons and studies, and the assumed prevailing culture which existed in the evangelical churches of which I was a part.

OUTCOMES

So how did the two studies go? Inevitably, it's rather awkward to comment on how the work you do is received, that's a judgement for others (or more likely your partner) to make. But in general, they went well. They probably erred on the side of being overly involved and detailed, but I had worked hard at preparing them and, although slightly nervous in my delivery, and especially declaring my own opinion, they were well-received by the majority. Perhaps I could have provided a summarized version alongside the notes I provided. Indeed, for some, these studies became the tipping point in their understanding. Whilst their lived experience might have caused some to incline towards a more inclusive position, all they had previously heard from the church was that such a lifestyle was incompatible with Christian truth. But here, perhaps for the first time, members were hearing of an evangelical rationale in favor of LGBT+ inclusion and it made sense.

5

What do our Church Members Think?

IRRESPECTIVE OF WHETHER OUR churches have engaged with the question of LGBT+ inclusion or not, whether there is a stated stance or not, whether we have open and known gay people in our congregation or not, the inevitability is that within our churches there exists a range of views about the matter.

I say this both from my experience at ABC, and also from conversations with members and leaders from other churches. There seem to be almost endless possible connotations of the positions people hold as they seek to translate their biblical/theological view into practical outworking. Whilst we seem inexorably drawn to caricature views and to put people in boxes, I have met conservative evangelicals who happily engage in discussion while others don't, and so-called progressives who still resist the idea of same-sex marriage.

As we began to look at the issue, both as elders and then as a whole church, it seemed helpful to assess where people stood on the issue. This would have several benefits. Firstly, it would help people gain clarity about their view. Hopefully this would be done with broad categories and without the result of straightjacketing people into categories which only approximated the view they held. Secondly, it would enable an individual to locate the view they held within a wider range of views, as such a template acknowledges that there are different views to the one that an individual holds. Finally, and perhaps this is the most valuable thing, such an approach might help us to see any incremental shifts we might take during the process and be clear about what those are and why we modified our view.

FINDING A STARTING POINT

Given the good work that had already been done by some of my Baptist colleagues, it seemed unnecessary to attempt to devise a new schema to detail the different positions people may hold on the issue. I was therefore grateful to Steve Elmes and Mark Elder who had already surveyed the possible views and done the legwork of formulating categories. Steve is a Baptist minister who has thought and written much about the subject, especially in the attempt to enable greater listening, conversation, and understanding on this issue. Mark, also a Baptist minister, is a member of the leadership team of Fresh Streams,[1] a movement of charismatic, evangelical Baptists who without giving a stated position, facilitated a summer school for church leaders to consider the different perspectives. Below I detail both the work of Elmes and Elder in order to give two possible options.

In his book, *Sexuality, Faith and the Art of Conversation: Part One*,[2] Elmes sets out five broad positions which might be held. These views can be starting-points, helping people to work out their initial position, whilst also being useful to people further through the process. Groups might wish to read them through and discuss which are the views they identify with; often people will not fit neatly into one box. They are summarized below:

1. The Bible condemns homosexual practice, and the church should always regard it as sinful. Furthermore, sexual

1. www.freshstreams.net
2. Elmes, *Sexuality, Faith, & the Art of Conversation*: Part One, 21–23

attraction to someone of the same sex should be repented of and healing sought from such desires.

2. The Bible condemns homosexual acts but says nothing about sexual orientation. Therefore, a celibate homosexual is no more sinful than a celibate heterosexual. However, it may be that, within the loving and caring support of the Christian community, a change of orientation might happen, opening up the possibility of heterosexual marriage.

3. The Bible's condemnation of homosexual practice seems to have in mind unloving acts which exploit others, e.g., rape, pederasty,[3] temple prostitution, and the search for illicit sexual thrills. It is therefore difficult to build a biblical picture of loving, faithful, committed homosexual practice. Perhaps people's orientation can change, but the idea that a good heterosexual marriage will bring about this change has caused many casualties which say otherwise.

4. The Bible's references to homosexual practice most likely refer to relationships which are unloving and exploitative. But it also says that in God's original purpose there is no alternative to heterosexual marriage, except celibacy. The Fall in Genesis 3 affected everything—including sexuality. Yet because God loves us and is working to redeem the whole of creation, could loving, faithful, committed same-sex relationships be one example of God's restoring work?

5. The Bible's condemnation of homosexual practice is aimed solely at unloving, exploitative acts and no prohibition is to be found concerning loving, committed and faithful homosexual relationships. God blesses such relationships as expressions of his purpose for humanity and the church should too.

In a similar way, Elder offers an alternative template. Although it suggests just four views, Elder gives greater detail in terms of

---

3. Pederasty: an erotic relationship between a man and a boy, socially accepted within Greek and Roman societies.

theology and ecclesiology, based on his observations of churches and conversations with their ministers.

Identifying and locating our position: How Baptist evangelical churches relate to gay people. *Gay—A generic term for lesbian or gay sexuality (Stonewall)*				
	Traditional Conservative	**Traditional Open**	**Inclusive**	**Affirming**
Approach to gay people who are celibate	Some sympathy, though "conversion therapy," under the guise of prayer ministry, practiced in some Pentecostal/ charismatic settings	Full acceptance and opportunity to serve so long as gay person remains celibate	Full acceptance	Absolutely full acceptance—a person's sexuality is a gift from God
Approach to gay people who are sexually active in a marriage or civil partnership	Need to repent before they can belong in the church family	Distinct unease but some sympathy	Genuine sympathy and (private) support	Unconditional welcome and support
Interpretation and application of Bible passages on homosexuality	Both OT and NT texts say that gay sexual relations are forbidden and incur God's judgment	Creation narrative and Pauline texts prohibit gay sexual relations	Revisionist view on various key texts that put loving, committed, gay relationships in different light	Look to the whole tenor of Scripture to uphold and affirm loving relationships of any type

How gay people view us	Don't go near or stay quiet about sexuality	Will still tend to keep sexuality private unless they are celibate	Those who are more courageous will be more vocal with the aim of shifting majority to affirming position	Feel a sense of belonging, unless they're living celibate lives out of conviction and then view affirming churches as liberal
View of the sacrament of marriage	Between a man and a woman	Between a man and a woman	Open to change to between two people who love one another	Between two people who love one another
Percentage of Baptist churches in BUGB	Significant number but decreasing (20–25%)	Significant number but increasing (35–40%)	Increasing number (20–25%)	Increasing number (15–20%)
Other mainstream denominations	RC; Anglican; Baptist; Pentecostal; Independent Evangelical (FIEC), New Churches (NFI, Hillsong, Pioneer)	RC; Anglican; Baptist; Methodist; Pentecostal; some New Churches	RC; Anglican; Baptist; Methodist; URC	Anglican; Baptist; Methodist; URC
Theological type: Reformed/ Arminian	Reformed; Arminian	Reformed; Arminian	Arminian	Arminian

WHERE DID ABC SIT?

In the years prior to 2022, I would have estimated that in broad terms ABC was split fairly evenly into three categories. Around a third of the church believed in, and would want to uphold, the traditional view that homosexual identity and practice were both wrong, or the view that, whilst homosexual orientation was not in itself wrong, acting on that inclination in thought or action was wrong. For this group, the question of LGBT+ inclusion was a line in the sand. To question this was an example variously of the continuing decline of society into sinfulness or the slide of the church into liberalism and anti-biblicism.

There was also around a third of people who simply didn't know or were unsure as to what they thought. Yes, they understood and appreciated the inherent view that ABC, as a "Bible-believing, evangelical church," probably should oppose the idea of accepting LGBT+ communities and practices, but they were torn. They had come to see examples of gay women and men who modelled good and godly characteristics. They had friends or work colleagues who were gay who didn't seem to fit the pejorative characterizations that some in the church had given them. And the world around them was changing and becoming more accepting, which meant it felt increasingly awkward to retain the view that people from these communities were still unwelcome within the church.

Finally, I would estimate that around a third of people at ABC would have considered that homosexual orientation or activity was not wrong and by implication would want ABC to change its inherent view on the matter. This group would include, I think, every person who had a family member who would identify as LGBT+. This is important to note. Whilst there are doubtless those in the evangelical world who retain a conservative/traditional view and therefore reject the idea that their gay son/daughter should be accepted as they are into the life and activity of the church, I did not find that to be the case within ABC. Every parent, brother, sister, aunt, uncle, or grandparent in ABC of someone from LGBT+ communities supported the idea of a revision of the church's view. And that was what we were discerning together—the church's view. Helpfully, Elder took his schema a step further and interpreted it for the whole church, giving his view of the five possible options for how the church might engage with the issue. This is especially helpful in cutting through some of the rhetoric and hyperbole which can obscure the issue. This, in effect, describes in practice how a church actually responds to those from LGBT+ communities.

1. The "ask no questions" option
   Gay individuals and couples are welcomed in the church because we choose not to ask too many questions about their status.

2. The "who are we to judge?" option
   The church is a "hospital" for wounded sinners rather than a community of saints. Therefore, who are we to judge when someone joins whose life is sinful? We should be removing the logs from our own eyes and not bothering about the specks in the eyes of others.

3. The "dialogue and discern" option
   The moral status before God of gay relationships is now uncertain or unsure in the Christian community. We need to carefully and sensitively engage in a conversation, a dialogue on this, akin to the "disputable matters" (Rom 14:1) of which Paul writes. This may or may not lead to a decision to live together in a forbearing and loving community, even if we don't agree on the matter.

4. The "pastoral accommodation" option
   Whilst God's original/best/intended plan was for lifelong committed monogamous marriages, the contemporary church is full of people who fall short of that plan. (For example, Matt 19 and Mark 10 hardly have in mind the high divorce rates we see today.) The church has been back-pedaling on this for years, and the pastoral response has been to meet such couples "where they are," even if it isn't God's best.

5. The "exclusion" option
   Refuse admission of any gay people into the church. So, when someone's child turns out to be gay, the issue can't be avoided, and they are exiled from the church unless they have committed to celibacy.

6. The "revised norm" option
Study the biblical texts, Christian tradition (theology) and the contemporary reality, and determine that the heterosexual-only ethic needs to be revised (the ultimate fork in the road).

At ABC we used the templates individually and privately as we were concerned that a show of hands might at this stage unhelpfully place people into groups and stymie openness and questioning. Perhaps we could have conducted some kind of private ballot, but that didn't occur to us as what we should do at that time. I share these templates as a tool to help a church leadership team or congregation gain clarity regarding the various positions which their members might hold, and to help establish the assumed position which the church holds. It became a useful starting-point for the exploration and conversations we were about to have.

6

Handling Critiques and Criticisms

It was the writer Adrian Plass who, in his own inimitable way, stated, "I hate all forms of criticism, especially the constructive sort." Criticism, though, is part and parcel of Christian ministry.

I recall once having a conversation with a Baptist Regional Minister (think bishop without the authority), where I suggested that, although I knew that holiness is perceived as being the key quality for a Christian minister, surely it had to be a grounded sense of one's own self-worth and the ability to take criticism. The word "criticism" originates from Latin and means the art of judging or defining the qualities or merits of a thing, as in "critique." It's only more recently that the meaning has shifted to mean disapproval. But when does a comment, a question, or a challenge become criticism? Getting to understand the difference between questioning and criticism is vital if one is to maintain one's sanity in ministry.

I recognized that, given the nature of the subject we were exploring, I was living with a degree of criticism as well as questioning. This would inevitably mean that I was likely to be sore, a bit more sensitive. I was entering a highly contested field—and especially so for an evangelical—and I needed encouragements, positive affirmations and comments which would motivate and spur me on. I did receive those, plenty of those and indeed, the repeated support I had from a range of people across the church was ultimately the energy I needed to complete the discernment process. But I wasn't without my critics.

They too were under similar pressure. Those who had little or no interest in engaging with the process, and who indeed might want to thwart or stymie what was happening, were fearful. They were fearful of seeing ABC, the church of which they had been a part for ten, twenty or more years, potentially changing its view on a subject they considered fundamental to a Christian lifestyle. As I have already stated, all of us were still adjusting to post-pandemic life. The world was a different kind of place, with many still grieving either the loss of a loved one or simply coming to terms with the uncertainties we had lived through. I was also confronted by the anxiety felt by those, most likely in the middle-ground, who had seen some people resign and leave. One person expressed it quite straightforwardly to me: "Ashley, I just couldn't bear it if one more person resigned from ABC."

I asked myself whether the criticism I began to face was necessarily wrong. After all, every football manager, school principal and politician faces criticism daily. Critique is necessarily a part of the process, but I think it can drift into criticism, when the spirit and motivation behind it is designed to belittle, or obstruct, or hurt. The church leader needs to recognize that both they and the questioner are likely to be processing much and feeling levels of uncertainty, and therefore must be clear about whether this is just tough questioning or something more pointed.

From all the critique and criticisms I received, it may be helpful to identify those which were perhaps the most emblematic and oft-repeated, to give some idea of the questions which are likely to come when undertaking this process. I list them in no particular order, and you, the reader, are free to consider their merit.

FORENSIC ANALYSIS

I received some long emails over this time. The church has many professional people who have sharp and able minds and could at the very least keep up with my level of understanding on the subject and in some cases exceed it. Some of these people sent me long emails citing historical context, definitions of Greek words and wider theologies of gender and marriage. In essence, they were doing exactly what I was doing. Was this a problem? No, it wasn't a problem at all. It may mean I would take an awfully long time to reply to some of these emails, but they were written with good intentions, a deep concern for the church and from a keen intellect. Replying to them fully was my responsibility.

On more than one occasion, people told me that at some point in the near future it might well be necessary for them to leave the church. This was both from people who held an affirming view as well as a traditional one. Was this blackmail, a strong-armed tactic to corner me into a certain reaction that would appease them? It certainly concerned me, but I nonetheless maintained that there was a greater goal for me and the church, i.e., discerning God's mind on this matter. I had not heard of any church that had emerged unscathed from this process, and it would perhaps be foolish to assume that it could be undertaken without such departures.

Amongst those who at least had reservations about engaging as we were with this issue was a retired man from Northern Ireland who had lived through the disagreement, division, and armed conflict which had characterized the country for forty years. Previously, he had been a member of the eldership team, and he was known for his equitable and gentle manner. He was a thoughtful man, a student of the Bible, and someone who loved God, people, and the church. Although concerned about the issue he hadn't spoken with outright opposition, and he had faithfully attended the *Creating Sanctuary* course and the Bible studies. So it was that one member who, aware of his views, asked him outright about his patient and engaged approach to what we were doing. His reply, given with a wry smile, was disarming: "You have to understand that until recently I had lived all my life in Northern Ireland, and if there is one thing we have learned over that time, it's that we have to keep talking to each other."

TIMING

Over this time, I was confronted with the repeated refrain, "This is the wrong time to be looking at this." In a sense that was true, it wasn't the best time. We were emerging from the once-in-a-lifetime experience of a pandemic. People's emotions had been tried and there existed a malaise across the church which would take time to overcome. This had doubtless been in the minds of the elders when it was decided that the conversation would be deferred. But I was acutely aware that delay was also avoidance of the issue and by avoiding it we were saying it wasn't *that* important, and we were not serving well those who were directly impacted by our silence.

It was also put to me that the Baptist Union had announced that it would undertake a consultation about whether gay ministers could marry and continue in their roles, something which is disallowed by Baptist ministerial rules. The consultation would be undertaken throughout much of 2023. So why do we have this discernment process now? Why not wait until we know the outcome of the consultation? I had much less time for this view. We were a church which was free to determine our own view on the matter. Irrespective of what the consultation decided, we could take an alternate view. This felt much more like filibustering, attempting to delay the process and deny us the opportunity of addressing a pressing issue.

DISTRACTION

Another criticism I received was that this issue was a distraction, taking us away from what was "the real work of the church." In essence, some were saying that this issue did not merit the time and attention we were giving to it and there were more important matters about church life and ministry which were being neglected, albeit that I don't recall people defining what these neglected areas might be.

The church had made a tremendous response to the pandemic. We had seen our work in the community grow and develop in new and unforeseen ways. We gathered online for weekly Bible studies and for Sunday services. Children's and youth work simply expressed themselves in new ways, and the care of the pastoral team meant that nobody was left behind. It felt as if more than ever we were fulfilling the call of Romans 12: 11–13 as Eugene Petersen's translation puts it: "Don't burn out; keep yourselves fueled and aflame. Be alert servants of the Master, cheerfully expectant. Don't quit in hard times; pray all the harder. Help needy Christians; be inventive in hospitality."

In terms of the importance of the subject, I can only reiterate the points I made in Chapter 1. This issue was the "background noise" for the lives each of us were living. For some people in the church, this was a deeply personal and significant issue, which continued to be a source of pain and distress. In terms of time and attention *vis à vis* other aspects of church life, I don't recall any staff team member or ministry leader expressing to me that their activity was undermined or obstructed by what we were doing.

AN AGENDA

This is when some say that "There's an agenda afoot," or "This is a woke agenda," or even, "This is just Ashley's agenda." What people seemed to be inferring by this was that beneath the apparent measured and thoughtful approach to the subject, there was a hidden agenda about which the outcome was already determined, and the church was simply being led to that conclusion. As I have previously said, I had for several years been forming and reforming my views on this subject and, at the outset, was participating in a process for my own benefit as much as for the church's. When it came to the Bible studies, I was expressing the conclusions I had reached at that point, so there was nothing hidden from the church. We were also subject to the Baptist method of decision-making, with its "democratic" voting by the members to determine issues. Ultimately, it would not be me or the elders who had the final say on the subject—it would be determined by all the members together.

DIVISIVE

This was an interesting one. The criticism was levelled that it was wrong to bring this for discussion because the issue itself was a "divisive issue." This made me think, a lot. It is obviously factually true that there are people who have differing views on this subject. But what people were suggesting was that there was something inherently malevolent, hostile even, in the subject, which was a reason why we shouldn't be addressing it. I certainly didn't want to be divisive and was working hard to bring the church together and include everyone, but was I kidding myself? Is the issue itself to be avoided because it divides people?

I thought about other so-called "divisive" issues—politics, sport, climate change, Marmite! All these things divide opinions, and yet having such different opinions on them is not wrong. The problem (divisiveness, if you like) emerges when we allow ourselves to become particularly agitated about these issues. Such agitation, though, is a choice. As with our Northern Irish member, it was evident that you could have reservations about having the discussion, or strongly hold a view at either end of the spectrum, but that didn't mean you had to be agitated or get angry about defending an interpretation of the Bible. But did it mean that you could still relate (be in fellowship) with someone who held a different view from yours? That was a question we addressed when we finally came to a mind on the issue.

When questioned about defending the Bible, founder of the Salvation Army, William Booth answered, "Defend the Bible? I don't defend the Bible. I simply let it out of its cage and let it defend itself!" That's what we were trying to do and, although the issue divides opinion, it would only become antagonistic and *divisive* if we let it.

"A SLIPPERY SLOPE. WHERE DO YOU DRAW THE LINE?"

This was the domino argument. If this, then what is next? If we were to change our mind on this question, then surely everything about sexual ethics is open to change. I was asked this question straight out, so I answered it "straight out" and explained to my questioner where I drew the line. I said that I didn't think it was a slippery slope; in fact, I reassured them that there were no other issues we were planning to look at. As for drawing the line, I said I drew the line at pornography and at fornication (sleeping around), pre-marital sex and serial monogamy. I drew the line at affairs and marital unfaithfulness. I drew the line at abuse in marriages of the emotional, verbal, violent, sexual, or neglectful kind. I also said that from my reading of the Bible, God seems none too enamored with the idea of divorce.

The slippery slope argument was perhaps the one which came up most frequently. When you are in the moment, looking on and trying to form an opinion, this argument appears to have substance. Which indeed it may do. However, there are a couple of other perspectives which I think should be stated to form a more accurate picture.

The first is the perspective which looks back on the past fifty years or so and acknowledges all the other changes that have occurred which at the time were considered to be a "slippery slope.." Take for example divorce, or divorce and remarriage. I was a teen in the 1970s and this was a significant issue, the kind of thing my parents would reference in hushed tones. While it didn't carry the scandal of the early twentieth-century divorce and especially the remarriage of a divorcee, divorce was deemed by many to be beyond the instruction of Scripture and thus a slippery slope.

Or what about Sunday Trading? In 1986, the Shops Bill was defeated in the UK Parliament, which would have brought a relaxing in the law regarding retailers opening on Sundays. The defeat of the bill was due in no small part to the Keep Sunday Special campaign, devised and run by evangelical businessman

Dr Michael Schluter. In evangelical churches across the land, sermons were preached, letters written, and protests made to defeat the bill. However, eight years later, the Sunday Trading Act was passed, permitting buying and selling in ways which were previously unlawful. Now, almost forty years later, there seems to be not the slightest embarrassment between me and another church member if I bump into them in the local supermarket straight after the Sunday service.

We could also speak of the limited place now of teetotalism within the evangelical church, our increased engagement with Roman Catholics in local "churches together" groups, the decline in a fundamentalist/creationist interpretation of Scripture and, of course, the ordination of women into ministry in evangelical churches as all being examples of how hitherto fundamental tenets of evangelical belief and practice were transgressed. My point is whether *this* step—the welcome and full inclusion of people from LGBT+ communities—is a slippery slope, or whether from our limited perspective, and without recourse to our recent history, it simply appears to be?

The second perspective is the one that challenges the view that the inevitable trajectory of Christian faith and practice is downward; after all, you can't slip *up* a slope. Those of a more conservative view might wish to cite the above changes as evidence of this, although I suspect the ending of hat-wearing by women may figure less significantly in their argument. How about then, the possibility that the trajectory of the church is not downward, but upward? If so, what evidence might there be for this?

In the Introduction, I shared something of my own story, growing up as I did in a wonderful and strongly Christian family for whom life revolved around Christian faith and church attendance. However, within that, I admitted to what we might now call the casual racism of that time which impacted my own family. Thankfully, to a large degree, those days seem to have passed, and certainly my own children and nephews would hotly contest any words or actions which had the whiff of racism. We now enjoy a far greater multicultural experience within church life, and the racism which was in evidence is being eradicated.

As a husband and especially as father to three daughters, I have experienced new perspectives on the identity and role of women in the church. These have given me insights into how women are treated both outside and within the church. My mother held various leadership roles before she was called to be a deacon, then elder, and also developed as a preacher who continued in this role into her seventies. My wife has, to a large degree, been spared the pressure to conform to the role of "minister's wife," with all its associated conventions. And my daughters have been free to work out their own faith, perhaps not so much with fear and trembling, but with curiosity, questions, and liberty of thought. Not insignificant to this was the development of "the five-pound rule." Picking up a prompt from a newspaper columnist who would often refer to his own family, my children were happy to adopt the rule that any reference to them in a sermon would necessarily result in a £5 note for whoever was mentioned. The hope was that this would either dissuade me from mentioning the kids, or at least sugar the pill when it did happen.

In the UK, the Baptists were the first mainstream denomination to ordain women (Revd Violet Hedger, 1926). However, the proportion of women being ordained as Baptist ministers remained woefully low for many decades. Nowadays, there are fewer and fewer Baptist churches which would resist the idea of having a woman as their minister, and very few indeed which wouldn't countenance a woman serving as a deacon or elder—a much-valued change in our church practice.

We might also cite the developments in biblical scholarship and theology which have served to improve our understanding over the past fifty years. Archaeological finds continue to add pieces to the jigsaw of biblical history. Textual criticism and the search for the historical Jesus have brought a greater appreciation of "Bible times" and have therefore impacted our evangelical understanding. In addition, the so-called "new perspectives" on Paul and his teaching on justification by E. P. Sanders, James D.

G. Dunn and N.T. Wright have made a major contribution to the atonement theology which lies at the heart of evangelical faith. Some will doubtless consider these developments to be distractions and subversions to a faith which is only truly defined and shaped by a reformed understanding, or by that which was forged by Christianity's response to the Enlightenment and the scientific age, therefore negating these developments. But it strikes me that these and other evangelical developments have only served to grow and enrich our understanding.

Finally, what about the pandemic? While I too staggered through those uncertain days, struggling to make sense of what I was experiencing, I did make time to read the guidance and perspectives given by significant biblical scholars. I read N.T. Wright,[1] Walter Brueggemann,[2] and John Lennox,[3] who helped me view this exceptional time through a biblical lens. All of them spoke of it being a honing and purifying time for the church, with the prevailing metaphor being that of Israel's exile in Babylon.

Of course, there will be some who staunchly resist the suggestion that the situations I cite and others are evidence for an improvement in church life, but I trust that the majority will recognize these changes as evidence of honing and improved health and vitality within the evangelical church.

UN-BAPTIST AND UNBIBLICAL

During the process, one email came the way of the elders describing what was happening as both un-Baptist and unbiblical. If you are not Baptist, please indulge me for a moment. I think the criticism was based on some old guidance, and guidance was all it was, that while each church is at liberty to discuss and determine its mind on any matter, it asked that churches hold fire in discussing this particular matter. However, around that time I had conversations

1. Wright, *God and the Pandemic*
2. Brueggemann, *Virus as a Summons to Faith*
3. Lennox, *Where is God in a Coronavirus World?*

with both our Regional Minister and the General Secretary of the Baptist Union (BU), both of whom confirmed that they had no opposition to us pursuing the matter. Also, there were obviously increasing numbers of churches who were having this very conversation, and indeed our discernment process was happening at a time when the Baptist Union's guidance was being reviewed. The consultation which the BU is undertaking is an invitation for every Baptist church to have the conversation.

Unbiblical? Being biblical is about choosing the Bible to be authoritative and definitive in one's life and understanding. It is taking the Bible and its story seriously, as the story which defines all our stories. But such an important thing easily gets twisted to the idea that "My interpretation of the Bible is biblical, but your interpretation of the Bible is not biblical"! There are many assumptions that are made when bringing the criticism that something is or isn't biblical, and these needed to be unpacked and addressed before the "it's not biblical" criticism might be seen to be valid.

At times it felt as if once you had addressed and answered one criticism, the person simply shifted to another—a bit like the thief who, coming across a set of keys, tries one after another to find the one which might unlock the door. It felt as if some were trying to catch me out, something which especially came from those wanting to comment to me or the elders on the issue, but not engage with the wider church in discussion. Whilst I had respect and time for genuine questions and challenges, there were times when I felt the heart behind what I was being asked lacked the qualities found at the end of Ephesians 3:

> Let no evil talk come out of your mouths, but only what is useful for building up, as there is need, so that your words may give grace to those who hear. And do not grieve the Holy Spirit of God, with which you were marked with a seal for the day of redemption. Put away from you all bitterness and wrath and anger and wrangling and slander, together with all malice, and be kind to one another, tender-hearted, forgiving one another, as God in Christ has forgiven you.[4]

4. Eph 3:29–32

ANTIDOTES

If these were the critiques and criticisms which I was facing, there also seemed to be no lack of antidotes to them. Through daily prayer, engagement with others and self-discipline, each and every criticism can be addressed in a way which is honoring to both God and the Christian community. This is what I found helpful at the time.

ELDER AGREEMENT

Working with the eldership team of the church was essential. In practice, this meant talking through and agreeing every significant step in the discernment process. The truth of the oft-quoted African proverb, "If you want to go fast, go alone. If you want to go far, go together," is lived out in this issue. Listening, explaining, taking a step backwards in order to take two forwards, are all crucial to ensuring that you move together as a team. Being able to communicate as a whole eldership throughout the process sends the significant message to the church that those appointed and entrusted with responsibility for vision and direction were in agreement about what was happening.

TRANSPARENCY

It won't be right to give a Hansard-like record of every comment made in elders' meetings or private conversations, but making available as much information as you possibly can helps to bring clarity and defuse suspicion.

ADMIT ERROR AND LIMITATIONS

At points I got things wrong, or at least stated points as certain when in reality they remained open to question. This was especially true in reading the long emails which I was sent where, on further examination, I discovered that my certainty on a particular point was misplaced. Paul confesses that at times he does the very thing he wishes he didn't[5] and so too I/we should not be slow to admit our own error.

RECOGNIZE THE MERIT IN THE OPPOSING VIEW

Taking a lead from the book *Two Views on Homosexuality, the Bible, and the Church*[6], the four authors who express differing views do at least recognize the merit they see in the alternative argument. Doing this builds trust and brings benefit when wanting to share one's own view with another; you will get a better hearing.

RECOGNIZE ALL POINTS OF VIEW AS VALID

Whilst you may not agree with every view proffered or every position stated, it is important however to recognize that someone's view is faithfully and earnestly held and is to be respected. Belittling the views of others is an especially unhelpful trait, and I am grateful to those in the church who modelled this in all their engagements.

MEET WITH PEOPLE, SPEAK WITH PEOPLE

This is an important and essential practice. It is recorded that poet and Church of Wales minister, R.S. Thomas, would at times cross the road in the towns in which he ministered to avoid members of his congregation, and that Alfred Wainwright would occasionally seek out a rocky outcrop in the Lake District fells so he could hide while other hill walkers passed as he preferred his own company. Whilst we might recognize the temptation to do this (after all, who relishes the prospect of facing further criticism?), as church

5. Rom 7:15

6. Loader, Defranza, Hill, Holmes, *Two Views on Homosexuality, the Bible, and the Church*

leaders we are not afforded this option. Engage, engage, engage. It's really demanding, but it is the essential graft required to faithfully undertake the process.

FORGIVE

For if you forgive others their trespasses, your heavenly Father will also forgive you; but if you do not forgive others, neither will your Father forgive your trespasses.
Matt 6:14–15

Forgiveness requires a focus on us, and is more to do with our choices than we might at first realize. Forgiveness is doing what is in our power to achieve in order to release us from bondage to anger and resentment. At times I was hurt, angry, or frustrated by what people said or how they acted. But without the possibility of sitting down with another person with whom tensions had existed and talking ourselves back to a place of ongoing relationship, the process would inevitably unravel.

It would be disingenuous for me to say that I faithfully fulfilled to the utmost degree all these antidotes to the criticisms I received. I didn't. It was hard, and demanded a greater strength of character than I possess. But these were the lessons I was learning, and they presented me with the means to stay on track, maintain perspective and finally complete the process.

7

How (Baptist) churches do doctrinal difference

I'M NOT A BAPTIST, GET ME OUT OF HERE!

IF YOU ARE NOT Baptist, this chapter might seem rather irrelevant, but hang on for just a moment. Whilst I want to look at the process for how doctrinal difference gets aired, discussed, and resolved in a Baptist setting (and this is likely to differ if it's not your denominal affiliation), the issues and contested areas remain the same. Your setting may be episcopalian, where you have bishops and a more hierarchical structure for decision- making on important issues. If you are presbyterian, you most likely have an elected committee of elders to decide matters. But if congregational (like the Baptists), then a much flatter form of governance is exercised. Although practiced by a minority of churches, the congregational approach places the discernment process and ultimate decision-making within a local church and in the hands of the members.

So yes, this chapter may sound a little strange to some, given the level of participation of a Baptist congregation in the decision-making process, and the fact that Baptist church members each have a vote to determine the outcome. But whatever denominational practice is yours, there is likely a place in each form of governance for people to meet in order to think, listen, pray, and debate. Many of the lessons we learned regarding *how* doctrinal differences are debated and decided upon are generic to the nature of the people of God.

HISTORY LESSONS

Understanding our church history can also be a rich vein for learning about how we might work with each other to a discerned position. Looking back can also deliver us from thinking that what we are currently facing is somehow a unique moment where the lines of division have never previously been drawn so starkly. This is not a unique moment, and church history shows us how previous issues have precipitated even greater divisions (just Google "Jan Hus" and "defenestration"). Controversy, disagreement, and the threat of schism has dogged the church for the past two millennia, and each generation, or so it seems, has had to wrestle with the pressing issue of the day.

Much of what I am about to share comes from *Something to Declare*,[1] an online resource explaining the history of the Baptist Declaration of Principle. I am also indebted to Revd Dr Ruth Goldbourne, whose excellent presentation, "When Convictions Clash, Can We Hold Together?"[2] helps bring color and insight to the past and points to the lessons which we can learn for today.

Unlike most other denominations, the Baptists are not unified around a creed or statement of faith. In fact, Baptists gather around, and are united by, a remarkably brief statement, known as the Declaration of Principle, the basis of the Union.

The Basis of the Baptist Union is:

1. *That our Lord and Saviour Jesus Christ, God manifest in the flesh, is the sole and absolute authority in all matters pertaining*

1. Fiddes et al., *Something to Declare*, 1996

2. Goldbourne, "When Convictions Clash, Can We Hold Together?," https://www.youtube.com/watch?v=uQr_gWIvruA

to faith and practice, as revealed in the Holy Scriptures, and that each Church has liberty, under the guidance of the Holy Spirit, to interpret and administer His laws.

2. *That Christian Baptism is the immersion in water into the Name of the Father, the Son, and the Holy Spirit, of those who have professed repentance towards God and faith in our Lord Jesus Christ who 'died for our sins according to the Scriptures; was buried, and rose again the third day'.*

3. *That it is the duty of every disciple to bear personal witness to the Gospel of Jesus Christ, and to take part in the evangelisation of the world.*

Brief though it is, it was first introduced in 1873 with the intent of holding together Baptists with differing theological understandings and the story of its formation can help us see how discussion, debate, and discernment about our beliefs and practices has played out in history.

It is the year 1608, which is generally credited with the genesis of the Baptist denomination, when the early Baptists separated from Anglican parishes due to the persecution they faced in rejecting infant baptism in favor of "believer's baptism." At that time, many early Baptists (Separatists) fled to Holland to avoid this hostility and there they were exposed to, and adopted, an Arminian understanding of faith. These Baptists then returned to England around the year 1612 and defined themselves as General Baptists, so-called because they believed that salvation was openly available (general) to all people and not specifically a distinct and predestined group (the Calvinistic view). However, a Calvinist understanding of salvation was also owned by other Baptist Christians who were consequently referred to as "Particular Baptists," believing that only a particular group were predestined and therefore could be saved. By the 1640s, these Particular Baptists had grown significantly in number and began to exert greater influence within the Union. Here we find some echo of a similar theological difference to that with which we are concerned today.

Over the next 200 years, the General and Particular Baptists continued to maintain their Arminian or Calvinistic identifies, whilst also seeing themselves as in some way bound together through their Baptist practice of believer's baptism. However, in 1812, there was a move by Particular Baptists in London to invite closer union in order "to promote the cause of Christ," which especially related to the Baptist Missionary Society and Baptist colleges. But—and here's the point—the proposed constitution stated that it "disclaims all manner of superiority and superintendence over the churches. . .." What this means is that whilst this constitution attempted to gather churches together under a set of beliefs, they did not wish to create a hierarchy which would deny each church its independence and freedom of conscience in matters of faith—a delicate balancing act!

Agreement was not forthcoming and yet it indicated the intention for Baptists to relate more closely together and to work together to serve the cause of Christ. So, in 1835, there was a new attempt to unite churches, again with "superiority and superintendency" rejected. But this time, the list of doctrines which a church must subscribe to had been removed and replaced with, "those who agree in sentiments usually denominated Evangelical." So, the basis by which these churches would relate was less about doctrine but more to do with mutual support and shared activity.

In the middle of the nineteenth century, there was once again a sense amongst some that there needed to be a more robust Union. So, in 1872, when a new constitution was drafted, the debate once again emerged as to a possible set of beliefs which would unify all Baptists. A proposal was brought to the National Assembly but again they rejected the Confession of Faith, settling on the understanding that each church be free to independently determine its beliefs. The covenant they agreed the following year is set out below. It is worth noting that at the same time, an additional six objects (goals) of the Union were also agreed, namely:

1. *To cultivate among its own members respect and love for one another, and for all who love the Lord Jesus Christ.*

2. *To afford opportunities for Conference, for the public declaration of opinion and for joint action on questions affecting the welfare of the churches and the extension of the denomination, both at home and abroad.*

3. *To promote fraternal correspondence between Baptists in this and other countries.*

4. *To obtain accurate information respecting the organizations, labors, and sufferings of Baptists throughout the world.*

5. *To confer and cooperate with other Christian communities as occasion may require.*

6. *To maintain the right of all men everywhere to freedom from disadvantage, restraint, and taxation in matters purely religious.*

Perhaps in that last statement we find a hint of the motivation behind avoiding a statement of faith. Having emerged from the Anabaptists of the Reformation who, amongst other things, rejected the rule of the Roman Catholic Church and were persecuted for their practice of believer's baptism, the Baptists would treat with great suspicion the idea that there would be "superiority and superintendency" over others, and that matters of belief be codified in such in a way which might deny freedom of conscience.

DECIDING TO SPLIT

Famed Baptist preacher C.H. Spurgeon, fearing that Baptists would be contaminated by a non-Reformed theology, adopted a robustly conservative tone, refusing to share any platform with those who disagreed with him. He propagated his views throughout the 1870s and 1880s through letters in journals, the social media of the day. This culminated in 1887 with the publication of three, unsigned, articles in Spurgeon's own publication, *The Sword and the Trowel*, in which it was stated that salvation theology was being "downgraded," and that the "perceived apostasy of the 18th century was being repeated." Pulling no punches, the articles also explained that some had "invented a new theology that was no more chalk than cheese," with the result that it was "making not disciples but infidels." Such was the impact of these articles that they were discussed in the national press. Spurgeon also made it known that he was considering leaving the Baptist Union.

By the end of October 1887, and despite attempts at reconciliation, Spurgeon had resigned from the Union stating, "To be very clear, we are unable to call these things 'Christian Union'; they being to look like Confederacies of Evil." Although Spurgeon left the Baptist Union, surprisingly few others followed suit, certainly not as many churches as he had hoped.

In 1888, there was a move to reconcile. The Baptist Union Council drew up a Declaratory Statement to be appended to the Declaration of Principle, which was adopted by the Council in April. Whilst offering an olive branch to Spurgeon, his response was that he wanted more, an evangelical statement of faith for the Baptist Union. Attempts to rewrite the statement to be acceptable to Spurgeon were unsuccessful and were, after all, rejected by the Assembly, since people were unwilling to concede to Council the power to issue a statement that would be binding on all churches. This was the proving ground of the Declaration of Principle, and it has remained the Basis of the Union ever since, with the Union riding the wave and emerging stronger as a result.

In 1891, came the formal amalgamation of the General and Particular Baptists. Although the differences in theology of salvation remained, they recognized they had more in common, and so their basis of union in Christ was enough to outweigh their disagreement. Despite this move for unity in the late nineteenth century, the Declaration once again came under pressure. This time it was the advent of biblical criticism, a more scholarly approach to studying the Bible, which caused divisions. This was the post-Enlightenment scientific age where Darwin's *Origin of the Species* (1859) had redrawn categories of understanding regarding Genesis' creation account. This heralded the rise of liberal theology in other denominations, especially within the Congregationalists with whom Baptists had previously had strong links.

(NB. In 1904, an addition was made to the Declaration namely, *"That it is the duty of every disciple to bear personal witness to the Gospel of Jesus Christ, and to take part in the evangelisation of the world."*)

THE IMPERATIVE OF RELATIONSHIP

The basis for the union of Baptist churches is therefore not a set of beliefs, but rather an agreed unity of relationship simply around three matters: where authority in the church lies, believer's baptism and the responsibility for personal witness by every member. Authority was not to be found in the pastor, the crown, or the wider church, but rather "in the people under the authority of Christ."

The rejection of a statement of faith, something aligned to the Apostles' or Nicene Creeds, was based on the historical experience of a denomination which was persecuted for its rejection of believer's baptism and consequent rejection of the idea that a body, Christian or otherwise, might be granted the authority to define the beliefs of individual churches.

Therefore our (Baptist) union together is covenantal, i.e., it is built on relationship as seen in the theology of early Baptists who developed a doctrine of a covenant, whereby a congregation might "walk together and watch over one another." Local congregations may determine that they should include a statement, or confession, of faith, but this was not a requirement. This is worthy of reflection. While we might be quick to draw lines of distinction and division based on beliefs and creeds alone, this would be a negation of the Christian truth that our practice of faith is even more important. Jesus' statement, "By this everyone will know that you are my disciples, if you have love for one another"[3] remains the defining characteristic of Christian living and must not be ignored, especially in this discussion. All of this brings to mind

---

3. John 13:35

the brilliantly titled seminar at a Proclamation Trust conference I attended many years ago: "See How These Evangelicals Hate One Another." Whilst tongue in cheek, it touched on a sore nerve that many of us will recognize.

PERMISSION TO DISCERN TOGETHER

Of course, this left open the issue of what might happen when significant theological disagreements arose. But rather than refer to a set of doctrines, the commitment of the Baptists was to discerning together the purposes of Christ, as revealed in Scripture. This takes the focus away from the academics, legalists, or any church hierarchy, and requires that our attitude and motivations play a significant part in determining the outcome. It forces us to ask questions, such as, "Did we overstep the mark and do we need to be repentant of what we said or how we said it? How careful are we of our use of language?" As in a married relationship where heavy words can all too easily be thrown around, our engagement with those with whom we disagree needs to be marked by control and grace.

Such a way of being denies us the possibility of retreating into our own bunkers at the first whiff of disagreement, but rather causes us to engage and to recognize and affirm all we can in the argument of the other as we work to maintain unity. It means not taking ready offence, even when offence might be meant. It means asking for clarification where uncertainty exists in one's mind, so as not to misinterpret or misrepresent the views of the other.

It also means that the emphasis should not be on asking each member what *they* think. We are "discerning the mind of Christ" and we are doing this together, not as individuals. The final casting of our vote can therefore only be made with full understanding and recognition of the engagements and conversations which the whole body participates in. Sometimes I wonder whether discernment is understood as being, "I'll go home and think about this, as well as having a little pray about it, then I'll come back and tell you what I think." The language and intent should always be corporate, and listening to each other has as much, if not more, significance

than expressing our own view. That is why it is to be greatly regret-
ted when not everyone participates in the process. We are lessened
by this.

Of course, this can only come at a price and one's own view
will be subordinate to that of discerned understanding of the whole
church. This approach resonates with that of Ruth Haley Barton
(see chapter 3). Authority, in my experience, is evidenced when,
with winsomeness, one would speak to the gathering words whose
wisdom, and thus authority, is heard and recognized as such by
the whole church body. In these ways love, or perhaps better put,
the law of love and unity, are placed firmly in the center of our
decision-making.

This means that decisions are not made, nor influence ex-
erted, apart from the gathered community of believers. It does not
happen in isolation, by WhatsApp group, or through covert meeting, but only when we come together.

Turning once again to Scripture, these ancient and wise words
of the Apostle Peter, were not simply appropriate to our process,
but we were beginning to flesh them out in our discussions and
finding the merit in them as we began to appropriate and adopt
them in our practice.

> For this very reason, you must make every effort to support
> your faith with goodness, and goodness with knowledge,
> and knowledge with self-control, and self-control with
> endurance, and endurance with godliness, and godliness
> with mutual affection, and mutual affection with love. For
> if these things are yours and are increasing among you,
> they keep you from being ineffective and unfruitful in the
> knowledge of our Lord Jesus Christ. For anyone who lacks
> these things is short-sighted and blind and is forgetful of
> the cleansing of past sins.[4]

4. 2 Pet 1:5–9

LESSONS IN LOVE

In a winsome and defusing blog post,[5] missiologist Mike Frost helpfully places the inclusion debate in the wider context of his church's history.

> *I belong to a small Baptist denomination in Australia. We are a broadly evangelical association of churches, united by a set of core doctrinal statements but with plenty of room for interpretation on non-core beliefs. We highly value the autonomy of the local congregation of believers to interpret Scripture and determine their values and practices. We have been a pretty moderate bunch in the evangelical tradition of people like John Stott, if that makes sense.*
>
> *I have belonged to this family of churches for nearly 40 years and in that time I have had to endure my sisters and brothers engaging in a major controversy every decade or so.*

He cites previous battlegrounds of inerrancy of Scripture, ecumenism, the charismatic movement, and the ordination of women as precursors to the current debate in his denomination regarding whether to allow churches that affirm same-sex marriage to remain in the denomination. In addition, he sets this debate in the context of the priorities which the denomination has. They are committed to tripling the number of churches by the year 2050, so have set about shaping a vision, and a set of values and goals, to achieve this task through Christ. However, he concludes his post with these sobering words:

> *But instead of rallying to fulfil these bold visions for Christian mission, we're debating the ins and outs of how to expel a tiny number of churches that don't agree with the majority on yet another non-core issue.*
>
> *You'd think we would have learned by now.*

5. Frost, *Breaking up the Family*, 2021

8

Concluding the Process

A TURNING TIDE?

AFTER THE TWO BIBLE studies in May, we once again took a break for a month or so. The studies had been significant for many, but challenging to some. Making space at this point would give the necessary time for people to think through all they had heard and for conversations to happen in a variety of contexts across church life. It also meant that the elders could continue to assess the situation. The studies were crucial to our understanding of the issue and, whilst I had chosen that moment to voice my own opinion, I had also been careful to offer various interpretations of the passages. But after those Bible studies, an interesting and unforeseen shift happened within the church members.

Up to this point, the weight of opinion which had been publicly expressed had rested firmly in the traditional camp. The historic and conservative view had held sway, and therefore the opinion of those with an affirming view was rarely voiced and when it was, it was spoken with trepidation. After the Bible studies, this seemed to have reversed. I had it reported to me by one of the elders that some of those of a conservative view were now feeling nervous about expressing their opinion. The elder in question was the one who had played a very "straight bat" in the discernment process so far, and who knew a number of those with strongly traditional views and had opted out of attending the *Creating Sanctuary* course.

I guess it wasn't just that the Bible studies had caused this shift. Some people had now left the church because of the inclusion process—something which doubtless unnerved some traditionalists who remained and meant there were fewer voices maintaining this view. Ensuring the freedom and confidence for everyone to express their view was vital, and we needed to maintain that shared space for everyone.

At the suggestion of this particular elder, and agreed by the eldership, I was tasked with contacting all those who were known to hold the traditional view to record their comments and concerns, and report them back to the elders to ensure that this view would be represented in elders' meetings and our wider church gatherings. It would be quite a lot of work but in the cause of fairness of process I agreed.

There were three questions which would form the basis of the conversation, namely:

a. *How do you feel about how ABC is engaging with this issue?*

b. *What do you think are the best ways for the church to discuss and discern this issue?*

c. *What are your thoughts about the content of the Bible studies that were presented to the church?*

The pressure of time meant that I was only able to meet some of the people face to face, contacting most by phone. Then, over the ensuing elders' meetings, I reported back what people had said. However, this didn't work out as smoothly as intended. On hearing my reporting of these views, the elder who had initiated the idea was upset with me. Apparently, I was too frank in my reporting back of what people had said, too candid about the precise language they used, and he suggested that whilst they may be happy to speak with *me* as they did, perhaps they didn't want it reported back so plainly to the elders. I wasn't convinced. I had no interest in either sugar-coating what people said or making it sound pejorative. The elders wanted to understand how people truly felt about the process and the accurate reporting back of those conversations, free from redaction, was essential to this, albeit that some chose to express themselves in unfortunate ways. The elder who had suggested this now wanted me to water down what people were saying and how they were saying it, in a way which would soften and mitigate what they said to me. A relational gap began to emerge between us.

A COSTLY LOSS

Earlier, I referenced how important unity (not necessarily uniformity) is within the eldership team, but also the fact that, at one point, my relations within elders' meetings were pushed to breaking-point. This was that occasion. Up to this point, I and this elder had always worked very well together; in fact, I had (and have told him since that I retain) a genuine respect and affection for him. We had always been perfectly honest with each other, but somehow, sadly I think for both sides, we seemed simply unable to reconcile on this particular matter. Just before his term as an elder ended, he resigned and stepped down from the eldership and then a few months later, left the church—thankfully not without a long meeting over coffee and cake, where work could be done to mend some aspects of our relationship. It remains one of those Paul and Barnabas moments from Acts 15 where a sharp difference of opinion led to an unfortunate parting of ways.

Over the summer, we gathered together at the church once more to discuss what people had heard, what they were thinking and what questions were most pressing. It was the evening of one of those blisteringly hot summer days and, although we met in a cool space, numbers were low, perhaps between thirty and forty. After a very brief recap, and with everyone in possession of full notes, we broke into groups of six to eight, each with an elder, encouraging people "not to be in a group with the person you came with." We wanted groups to be as mixed as possible, in order to facilitate the greatest possible cross-fertilization of speaking and listening. After an hour or so, we heard a summary from each group of what they had discussed. I reminded everyone to keep thinking and praying and of course emailing me with questions or views.

Summer and the inevitable slowdown in church activity then ensued, and the discussions and profile of our inclusion discernment went quiet. September was once more the start of the "new year" for the church and, while we didn't forget the process, the regular calendar of church life became our focus. We would doubtless return to complete our discernment in the autumn, but it could wait for now. What we as an eldership team then decided was a product of our reflection on the process that had occurred to date. Those steps had been as follows:

- September 2021: The elders had agreed that the church would look at the issue of LGBT+ inclusion.

- February–March 2022: We undertook the *Creating Sanctuary* course.

- May 2022: Shared testimonies and Bible studies on the relevant Bible texts and passages.

- July 2022: The church gathered to discuss the issue.

The sense was that some in the church remained uncertain about what we should do, while others remained strongly opposed to any revision of the church's practice in this area. However, for most in the church, the greater inclusion and involvement of those from LGBT+ communities was something they either warmed to or was something about which they were strongly in favor.

Listening to the church, and understanding where the church was, enabled us to make good and appropriate judgements at each stage. Once again, the idea of setting out a comprehensive plan from the get-go would have been a clunky way to run the process. Amending and adjusting what happens is important. This also raises the question of whether from the start you need to give a clear goal, i.e., starting the process by clearly defining what the destination would be. I quite understand that there are few people willing to set off on a long journey uncertain of the destination. Whilst this might look like an adventure for some, it will appear a mystery tour for others, breeding fear and uncertainty. We had obviously given direction to the process—we were discerning our view on LGBT+ inclusion; however, we hadn't determined the precise destination. What ultimately was the question we would seek a decision on? If we had attempted to define that from the outset, it would have been alienating for some and would have left us committed to a timetable and set of statements which we would discover to be no longer appropriate.

WHAT IF?

In late September, I suggested to the elders that a helpful next stage would be for us to look at the practical changes for ABC were we to become an inclusive church. This would move us away from theological ideas to explore what might practically change in church life. Whilst this might sound quite logical, which in a sense it was, this felt for me like a shift away from the relative safety of ideas and opinions into the practical reality of how we might do church differently. I was aware of the numbers of people who had slowly drifted away from church and how this step might indeed precipitate a similar response. I was concerned about friendships and relations across the church and, to some degree, my own position within it. If, having led the church through so costly a process, the church was unprepared to follow this through, the level of trust the church had in me would doubtless bring into question my suitability to remain as Lead Minister. We agreed as elders to look at the practical implications, and set a date for 1st November. It felt like we were moving to the "business end" of the process.

I now had more work to do. I needed to work through the implications of all that we had previously thought about and considered, and now translate these ideas into the possible reality of full inclusion of those from LGBT+ communities in the life of ABC. It felt like we had come a long way from dipping our toe in the water with the *Creating Sanctuary* course. As I thought through the possible implications, it became clear that they would revolve around four key areas: baptism, church membership, church leadership, and marriage.

BAPTISM

Baptism is the initiation rite which marks the beginning of our journey in following Jesus. Of the fifty references to "baptize" or "baptized" in the New Testament, it's helpful to appreciate the ideas or context in which these words appear. All these references are in the context of "following Christ." Some explicitly refer to "faith" and some specifically refer to "repentance" or "confession of sin." These three aspects of baptism can be seen in our own "baptismal confession," which each candidate I baptize is invited to make. Each candidate is questioned about their faith (belief), Lordship (a determination to follow) and repentance:

- *Do you believe in one God, Father, Son, and Holy Spirit?* I do. This is the God who I trust.

- *Do you confess Jesus Christ as your Lord and Savior?* I do. He has saved me and called me by name.

- *Do you turn from sin, renounce evil, the devil and all his empty promises, and intend to follow Christ?* I do. Christ is my way; he is the truth, and he is my life.

Stepping back for a moment from the specific issue we are considering and looking at baptism in a wider context, it strikes me that the repentance part of baptism can at times morph into a judgementalism which manifests itself in questions like, "Are they repentant of all their sins?" and, "Do they have an absolute determination not to sin again?"

My understanding of baptism and repentance is rather more generic. Whilst someone may be cognizant of a particular sin or sins, it is recognition of our generic fallenness and resultant distancing from God which is to be acknowledged. Repentance is the prodigal's recognition of their failing, their separation from the father and their resolve to come home. Our old lives were characterized by sin (rebellion towards God), whereas the new life is characterized by obedience (peace with Christ). Therefore, we do not baptize now-fully perfect people—we baptize those who might still swear, love money too much and hang on to their resentments a little too tightly. We do not baptize people fully cognizant of all Christian truth—we baptize those who know and understand enough of the Good News to want it for themselves. We do not baptize now-fully "heart-in-tune-with-God" people—we baptize those whose hearts and wills have been so impacted by the Good News of God's love for them that they resolve to follow Jesus. If sinlessness of action, thought or heart-inclination were required for baptism, I don't imagine we would baptize anybody, let alone be baptized ourselves. Indeed, if we were to question every baptismal candidate about their possible love for career, wealth or self as a condition for baptism, we would likely refuse it to a lot more people than we would baptize.

Whether we believe same-sex activity to be sinful or not, it should not preclude us from baptizing someone. Subsequent transformation of whatever kind will come through the work of the Holy Spirit, the teaching of the Bible and the redeeming effect of the community, and while these will take time, we welcome and baptize those who wish to follow Christ (and affirm the statements we put to them). Therefore, the question of whether we should baptize those from the LGBT+ communities seemed to me to be a non-question.

CHURCH MEMBERSHIP

Church membership is peculiar to Baptist churches. Instigated in the Victorian era as a convenient way to define, manage and organize those who were committed to the church, Baptist churches reserve participation in leadership and decision-making only to those who have become members. Becoming a member usually involves a visit from the minister or an elder/deacon to ascertain the faith-story of the one wishing to become a member, and to explain something of the history, life, practices, and, these days, vision of the church they are wishing to join. So, in preparing the material I would share with the church, I returned to some core documents about membership, our constitution and the guidance given on the BU website. What was confirmed for me in doing this was that to become a member of a Baptist church, just three things are needed.

Firstly, a member is required to hold faith in Jesus Christ and a desire to follow Him. Essentially this is the earliest Christian confession: "Jesus is Lord."

Secondly, there is a commitment to join with these people here, *this* church. Baptist churches run their own affairs and have liberty to make their own decisions, so you are not joining a franchised branch of a conglomerate, but a locally gathered group of believers who have decided to opt in to a wider union of churches with whom we relate. It's those who sit around me and whom I serve that I am joining.

Finally, in becoming a member of a Baptist church, you are agreeing to do things in a Baptist way. We practice believer's baptism; we gather in church meetings to discern the mind of Christ, and we operate under the auspices of our Declaration of Principle.

Therefore, these three elements—following Jesus, joining with *these* people, and doing things the Baptist way—are the three requirements for membership.

The reason I state this so plainly, and was at pains to communicate to the church, is that unfortunately an attitude of vetting seems to have slipped into the process of becoming a member. As I mentioned in chapter 1 rather than simply employing these three conditions for local church membership, somehow other criteria (dependent on each church's or each person's view) have in some places become necessary.

The Baptist material on the matter is quite clear. These alone are the criteria for membership, but some people project onto membership additional conditions which reflect such personal views about who can become a member, or the misplaced belief that membership requires a certain level of sanctity. In this they are making two errors. Firstly, they confuse the invitation to become a member with the accountability and responsibility of being a member. It is only once someone becomes a member that other responsibilities of membership come into play. Within the standard Baptist constitution, there exists an unfortunate and decidedly ambiguous "normal responsibility" of membership which, misinterpreted as it can be, has become the basis of this vetting. It is the normal responsibility to "uphold Christian values" which has been misinterpreted as justification for such vetting. Whilst I understand the good intent behind the statement, it has two potential flaws. Firstly, it can and is used by some to be a condition of becoming a member. Therefore, any known or assumed "sin" can be used to judge the one wishing to become a member and disbar them from entry. It is clearly hypocritical to make such a judgement, unless as Jesus pointed out, you are without sin yourself. Sinlessness is not a condition of church membership.

Secondly, "Christian values" are of course open to interpretation, and therefore the good intent of this line is undone by its lack of definition. What are Christian values, all of them, a complete list? Does your list of Christian values agree with my list of Christian values? It's at this point that I recall the old rhyme, "I don't drink, or smoke, or chew and I don't go with girls that do." Perhaps this meant something in the Bible Belt of 1950s' America, but to our contemporary ears this sounds both sexist and old-fashioned. I was reminded of my great-uncle whose membership of his local church was removed after it was discovered that he owned a pack of playing cards! Whilst we can doubtless agree over many Christian values, we also disagree over many others. The judgementalism which Jesus so stringently opposes can creep into church life, and I wonder whether this is one of its doorways.

Separating membership from baptism also looks like a nonsense. David Pawson's *The Normal Chistian Birth* sets out a template of characteristics of becoming a Christian, of which faith, baptism, and joining the church are all essential aspects. To baptize someone but deny them membership would seem inconsistent.

CHURCH LEADERSHIP

We also considered how church leadership might look for an affirming Baptist church. Today we have many kinds of leaders in church. We have worship leaders, house group leaders, youth leaders, welcome team leaders. To talk of these different kinds of leaders is appropriate to our context today as it recognizes that people take important leading positions across the life of the church. However, the New Testament appears to talk only of two kinds of Christian leaders: elders (overseers) and deacons. So, we have a bit of work to do to try and join up the New Testament teaching on leaders and our own organizational understanding of leaders.

In surveying all the New Testament texts on leadership, three aspects emerge: character (what character is required to lead?), conduct (what actions are required of a leader?), and context (what is the necessary context from which a leader needs to come?). In essence, we can readily deduce that maturity of faith in understanding and practice is required for leadership, while "sinful behavior" is incompatible. Therefore, the matter of eligibility for Christian leadership is determined by our view of whether practicing same-sex attraction, transgender, or other forms of sexual or gender identity, is sinful or not, and determine whether we believe that a certain woman or man are suitable for church leadership.

MARRIAGE

Whilst we might well think that in the Christian world the "'institution" of marriage is one of those eternal and unchanging aspects of church life, something which is the same the world over, this is in fact far from the case. Our practice and understanding of Christian marriage have undergone significant changes over the past 2,000 years. These include:

- Expectations about the age at which couples get married.

- Where a couple is married, i.e., the home, a town hall, or the church.

- Understanding that the woman was "'owned" (a chattel) by the woman's father, an ownership which could be "given away" and transferred to the woman's husband.

- Whether a dowry is paid.

- How many wives a Christian man might have.

- Whether the woman promises to *obey* or *cherish* her husband—the shift from hierarchical to egalitarian marriage.

- Whether church leaders are allowed to marry.

- The introduction of contraception.

From the above list we might well conclude that whilst Christian marriage is enduring, it is certainly not unchanging. However, there is one aspect of the understanding of marriage that has until only recently remained unchallenged. This is of course the idea that Christian marriage is between "one man and one woman."

The enduring nature of this belief and practice remains significant in our collective understanding—so much so that it seems almost unnecessary to explain it. Suffice it to say that the basis for this understanding has been founded on the joining of Adam and Eve as found in Genesis 2:18–25. The permanence and uncontested nature of this view is also argued on the biological need for a man and a woman to participate in the procreative act, which is fundamental to the opening chapters of Genesis and therefore the joining of a man and a woman. Genesis simply doesn't cover celibacy, IVF, gender fluidity, the unwillingness or fear of having children, the desire for a partner but unavailability of a suitable one, a sexless marriage or those in LGBT+ communities. We therefore do violence to the Bible if we impose on it questions which were not in the mind of the authors, or their concern in writing.

One "inconvenient truth" of straightjacketing the text in this way relates to Genesis 1, and God's instruction to "go forth and multiply," which appears immediately after we read that "male and female he created them." In conversation with one of the authors of the Church of England's report, *Living in Love and Faith: Christian teaching and learning about identity, sexuality, relationships, and marriage*, I asked whether going forth and multiplying was a command and what therefore might be the implication of failing to obey such a command. He confirmed to me that it was indeed a command and therefore to not multiply, i.e., to marry and to decide not to have children, would therefore be sinful. (I decided not to ask about how *many* children being fruitful meant. Nor did I refer to my own Christian parents' concerns about starting a family in the early 1960s when the Cold War and Cuban Missile Crisis were at their peak and their consequent fears and hesitation about bringing children into such a world. Would that have been a sin as well?)

In looking at these four areas, we probed and examined some of our key beliefs and practices. These were historic teachings, things the church held dear, perhaps our "sacred cows." Whilst on occasion a church might have reason to review any one of these practices, we needed to look seriously at all of them and test whether our inherited interpretations and practices stood up to scrutiny as we searched the scriptures.

CONCLUDING THE PROCESS

Just over a week after we looked at these practical implications, we gathered again to discuss the input I had shared. We were now talking about things which had brought sober-minded focus to our considerations, yet once again the church did this with equity and respect.

In an elders' meeting two weeks later, we reflected on the latest input and consequent discussions. Whilst I was aware that we were moving towards a conclusion, I was still slightly surprised by the conclusion that the elders came to. There didn't seem to be anything more to say, in terms of input. We had prayed together, gathered, talked and listened together, and opened ourselves to be indifferent to all except what God was saying to us. And perhaps aware of the "drip-drip" of members leaving the church, the elders began to talk about the need to not unduly stretch out the process of discernment. And so, it was suggested that we come to a place of decision.

We were entering the busyness of Advent, then Christmas and the New Year—not the time to add in a further demand on the church. We already had a date set for our first church meeting in the new year, and so it was agreed that this would be the date when we would bring the process to a conclusion. The meeting on 9th February 2023 would finally determine the outcome.

9

What the Church Discerned

WHEN AND HOW WOULD WE MAKE A DECISION?

It was December 2022, and the year-long process was drawing to its conclusion. At the eldership meeting on the 5th, it was confirmed that the process was now at an end and it was time for a decision. For Baptist churches that means a Church Meeting, where each member votes to determine the outcome. Ordinarily, any vote is carried by a simple majority (i.e., more than 50 percent), albeit that usually much greater support is hoped for, ensuring that the church is united in the decisions it makes.

Baptist Church constitutions also have the facility for Special Church Meetings. These are convened when the matter at hand is of a greater magnitude. This would normally be exercised in the event of determining the appointment of a new minister and, indeed, for a matter as significant as the one we were considering. In holding a Special Church Meeting, various other factors came into play, including that the proportion of votes required to pass any proposal would have to be at least two thirds. Whilst I had been heartened by the response of the majority to the discernment process, I remained nervous about the outcome. Perhaps when the rubber finally hit the road, all that positivity might evaporate. What if the support for the proposals was less than two thirds, or perhaps more difficult, it was only just over two thirds? Wouldn't that still demonstrate that a significant proportion of the church were still against or at least unsure about such a move? Once again, the elders asked me to come up with some wording which, after further discussion and revision, could be brought to the church meeting planned for February.

As I have already stated, apart from the fact that we were discerning our shared understanding of how we might rightly include those from LGBT+ communities, we had no defined "destination" from the outset towards which we were working. To have identified a statement or statements from the start, which we would ultimately decide upon at a predetermined date, seemed unnecessarily presumptuous and constrictive. Whatever the church would ultimately decide would be shaped by the shared process, an evolving understanding, and what we took to be God's timing.

WHAT EXACTLY WERE WE DECIDING?

In broad terms, it seemed reasonably obvious what elements would make up the recommendations we would bring to the church for a final decision. There would be something about welcoming all kinds of people into the life of the church. We would specifically identify different ethnic groups, genders, and ages etc., alongside those from LGBT+ communities. We would state that those from LGBT+ communities would be welcomed as members of the church and would be able to take up positions of leadership across the life and activities of the church. It also seemed likely that we would also take the step of agreeing to perform same-sex marriages and would therefore register our building for such events.

The form of the proposed statements that we would bring also needed careful thought. Would we have statements which people could simply vote for or against (or abstain—which means the vote is not counted for or against), or should we have options, i.e., vote for option a, or option b. After some thought it seemed simplest and most helpful for people if we had straight statements which people could vote for or against.

Whilst Inclusive Church, a network of churches united around a shared vision of inclusion, has devised an "IC statement" which may constitute the nearest thing there is to an agreed form of words, it seemed that other churches had been inclined to create their own statements. Perhaps this is because this is still relatively new territory, or because of the lack of a clear roadmap for the process. The combination of the particularities of contexts and specifics of each church's process has meant that there appears to be no great consensus on the wording of final statements. In terms of coming up with precise wording, the websites of other churches which had become fully inclusive proved to be extremely helpful for gleaning wording and phrases which could form the foundation of our statements. Having spoken to other church leaders, each of whom welcomed the sharing of the wording they had devised (or borrowed themselves from others), I was able to construct a form of words which appeared right for us. These statements would have to be shared with the church well in advance of the church meeting to give people adequate time to discuss and prayerfully consider the proposals.

As I have previously stated, I thought I had a reasonably clear idea of what the statements would be. However, there would be one final twist. Amongst all the communications I had received, there were a few emails which, whilst broadly supportive of the discernment process, still expressed uncertainty or opposition to the idea of registering the church building for same-sex marriage, which I think had been an assumption in the minds of the elders and many in the congregation. The question this raised in my mind was further compounded by a chance conversation. Along with the church's ministry team, I am a regular attender at the annual Fresh Streams Conference, a gathering or around 300 (mainly Baptist) church leaders in the first week of January. At the conference in January 2023, I was delighted to bump into a friend and fellow minister I had known for thirty years. Steve

Elmes had already spent a long time considering the issue and the chance meeting meant we arranged to skip a conference session and have a talk.

CHANGING MY MIND

Discernment has many elements, but surely the most important is attentiveness to the Spirit and what he is saying. As Steve spoke, in his informed, disarming, and pastoral manner, I instinctively knew that God was using this conversation to shape what we were doing at ABC. Although Steve was leading his church on a similar journey and had expended much effort in this through writing his three books, as I listened to him, I felt I was hearing God's words to me, to *us*. Hearing God for a situation can be difficult and perhaps subjective, so why did this register so significantly?

Like Wesley's "strangely warmed heart," I sensed the resonance of what Steve was saying. Having placed great onus on God speaking and revealing His will during the process, I was convicted that, although this was a different path from the one I had envisaged, it was a path that amended the plan but didn't take us away from where we appeared to be being led. In truth, I didn't particularly like what God seemed to be saying; after all, I was by now convinced that same-sex marriage fell within the auspices of a Christian lifestyle, and that we should pursue this for our community. But once again "indifference" was the watchword. What I thought I was hearing was that now was not the right time for such a step. Once again, this needed to be a team decision, one which was agreed to by the elders and could be brought to the church.

So, the following week, I found myself back in an elders' meeting with the key agenda item being the precise wording we would bring to the church. I shared with the elders the conversation I had had at the conference and my belief that, whilst personally in favor of registering the church for same-sex marriage, now it seemed a step too far. I recall that whilst most elders supported this last-minute change to the expected wording, one elder was initially strongly opposed to the idea. We talked it through, each elder sharing their perspective and finally arrived at a place where we agreed not to push for a vote on registering the building for same-sex marriage. The dissenting elder wished that the proposal would provide facility for same-sex marriage but, alluding back to the guidance of Ruth Haley Barton and how we make decisions corporately, was happy to concede to the majority view. This, it seemed, was God's word to us at this time.

AGREEING THE WORDING

So, the wording was finalized and circulated the following day to the church for consideration. It was sent to all church members, with a covering letter detailing the date and nature of the Special Church Meeting in February. Reference was made to all the resources we had considered over the previous twelve months, including links to the Bible studies and generally available online videos which reflected the different views of the issue. We also proposed an amendment to our constitution. The pandemic had paused our ability to gather, not just for services but also for our church meetings. Decisions still had to be made but, after some Boaz-like fancy legal footwork by the Baptist Union, it was agreed that online voting was legitimate if all the decisions made at online church meetings were ratified in-person once they were finally allowed. Some churches had therefore considered changing their constitutions to allow online voting in perpetuity to enable those who were older, unwell, or away from home to still participate.

Motivated by the importance of this decision and the consequent desire to maximize participation, we proposed that, before the vote on inclusion, those present in the building would vote on whether to allow online voting into the future which, if agreed, would allow those online to participate in the discernment decision. It was anticipated that this would be most useful to some of our older members and perhaps members who might be more resistant to what was being proposed. Again, this seemed like an appropriate "check and balance" to ensure that the process was as equitable and fair as it could be.

Writing to the church members the statements we asked them to decide on were listed as follows:

- *Altrincham Baptist Church believes that all people are loved by God. We welcome people of all ages, genders, ethnicities, gender identities, sexual orientations, physical and mental abilities, neuro-diversities, education, classes, economic status, or political outlook.*

- *We welcome all people who are seeking to follow Jesus to participate in all areas of church life including baptism, communion, church membership, child dedication, leadership of mission and ministry, and eldership.*

- *We will warmly receive same-sex couples into our community to participate in all of church life.*

- *We commit ourselves to living graciously together in the community of Christ regardless of differences on these matters and call each of us to the love and grace which are fundamental aspects of the Christian community.*

We ended the letter with the following words:

> *In the week preceding the 9th of February, the elders are inviting the whole church to pray and fast—at least at some point. The elders have been encouraged over recent weeks by God's shaping of their understanding and consequently the statements which they now bring to the church. We very much value the input received from every person who has already contributed to this process and continue to be open to what God is saying.*
>
> *Also, the tenor and nature of the process has been marked by grace, listening, respect, and real concern for each other. This has been so helpful as it has enabled deep listening to each other and the Spirit. We look forward to this continuing as we gather on 9th February.*
>
> *So please take time to review the resources and especially watch the videos in the links. Pray and listen as the Spirit guides us individually and corporately and we look forward to seeing you at the meeting on 9th February.*

CHURCH FAMILY GATHERING

The 9th of February 2023 was almost exactly one year since we had started the discernment process with the *Creating Sanctuary* course, and two years since the issue two young women raised on a Sunday morning had become one which we could no longer ignore.

The day arrived, and attendance at the meeting was understandably high, as around a hundred members were present. The meeting was opened, as each one is, with a time of sung worship and prayer before we moved to the decisions we were to make. The Church Secretary explained the proposed constitutional change to enable online voting, which was passed unanimously. She then reminded us of the proposed statements and prayed. Voting slips were circulated in-person and online and people made their decisions. The papers were collected to be counted by two non-minister, non-elder, members of the church. Then we waited.

Television talent shows have overcome the awkwardness of vote-counting by having an advert break, or even a "results show" at another time. We simply invited people to turn to each other and have a chat. It took quite a time. Not only were there four different decisions being made, but adding up, checking and double-checking votes cast for, against and abstentions, along with calculating percentages to set against the two-thirds requirement to pass the proposals, all took a long time. Finally, a slip of paper was passed to the church secretary who called us to order and read the results. They were as follows:

1. *Altrincham Baptist Church believes that all people are loved by God. We welcome people of all ages, genders, ethnicities, gender identities, sexual orientations, physical and mental abilities, neuro-diversities, education, classes, economic status or political outlook.*

   For: 97 percent; against: 3 percent

2. *We welcome all people who are seeking to follow Jesus to participate in all areas of church life including baptism, communion,*

*church membership, child dedication, leadership of mission
and ministry, and eldership.*

For: 93 percent; against: 7 percent

3. *We will warmly receive same-sex couples into our community
to participate in all of church life.*

For: 83 percent; against 17 percent

4. *We commit ourselves to living graciously together in the community of Christ regardless of differences on these matters and
call each of us to the love and grace which are fundamental
aspects of the Christian community.*

For: 98 percent; against: 2 percent

The discernment process was now complete, and the church had
overwhelmingly determined to welcome those from LGBT+ communities into membership and any level of participation in church
life, save for ordained ministry. (As previously stated, the Baptist
Union still opposed the idea that a same-sex-attracted minister
could be married, and ABC would likely have to leave the Union if
it decided differently.)

Whilst we had hoped for unity's sake that there would be no
undue expression of feeling as the results were read out, there was
a spontaneous ripple of applause, and one whoop of delight. There
was prayer and the meeting ended, at which point some of those
who had been in favor of the proposals went immediately to con-
sole some of those who were known to oppose them.

Personally, there was an enormous sense of relief. Relief
mixed with disbelief. Whilst I had been hopeful that the church
would conclude in support of the proposals, the level of support
took me by surprise and, indeed, delivered the church from any
awkward uncertainty caused by a positive yet marginal approval
rate. I had a few brief conversations, and several people thanked
me for the part I had played, but emotionally I felt a combination
of being both elated and overwhelmed.

In my mind I replayed some of those difficult meetings and conversations I had experienced. I recalled some of the criticisms I had received and the times when my grace had been stretched to its limits. Mostly I recalled the names of people who had been crucial to enabling this outcome to happen.

WHY THIS OUTCOME?

The reasons for the overwhelming support seemed to be several. A significant number of those who held a conservative or traditional view on the issue had over the previous twelve months decided to leave the church and therefore were no longer members and had not voted. Also, we had held back from the proposal to register the building for same-sex marriage. This may sound like an inconsistency because of our welcome of same-sex couples into all areas of church life, but during the process we came to realize that perhaps these inconsistencies do exist at least for a time. But far more positively, there had been, for numbers of people, a shift in their understanding of the issue. This had been brought about through the testimonies, the conversations and, perhaps most significantly, the Bible studies and prayers. We had passed through this challenging time and had emerged as a church in a new place.

10

Counting the Cost (and Reaping the Benefits)

IN THE MONTHS THAT followed, the full cost of the discernment process and the decision we had arrived at were finally being counted. Jesus made it plain in Matthew 16 that following God's leading inevitably has a cost, and whilst already aware of some of the ways this would impact on the church, there would be others which would be a surprise. It was intriguing and at times challenging to see the multiple layers of impact that we would experience.

Although I have listed below the aspects of the process which seemed to be detrimental to the church, along with those aspects which were beneficial, this is something of a false dichotomy. For ease of reference, I present them as lists, but in practice, the cost is much more nuanced and visceral. In some ways, counting the cost involves statistics and numbers, but how do you enumerate the impact on hearts and relationships? And please don't see the process as being about weighing up pros and cons and opting for the least painful or most beneficial outcome. It's simply not like that. When you are in the process, it feels like a mix of both the costly and the beneficial all at the same time.

PEOPLE LEAVING

Ever since the first resignation on the issue when Mark 5 was preached on and applied in a way inclusive to those from LGBT+ communities, and especially throughout 2022, we saw people leave the church. Going back through the records of church meetings, where resignations are noted, I calculated that 23 adult members as well as 31 other regular attenders (including children) left through this time. In addition, a few people had simply started attending other churches while not yet resigning their membership at ABC. This may be because they simply hadn't got round to resigning, or indeed because it meant they could retain a foot in the door and keep an eye on what was still happening at ABC. Perhaps some can't quite bring themselves to take this ultimate step and in due course we will speak with them all with the aim of helping them come to a clearer mind.

One of the emotionally challenging aspects of this was the "drip, drip" of resignations. It was far from being the case, even when the decision was made, that people left *en masse*. As people left the church in ones and twos, the pain of these departures was drawn out over a long period of time. While some simply left the church without any conversation, others left only after some helpful engagement and conversation. In each of the latter cases, this was marked by grace and generosity of spirit between both parties, for which I am grateful.

I also wonder whether for some, their leaving of ABC was a good thing, for both parties. Whilst this issue had precipitated their departure, it had been obvious that for some their discomfort at ABC had been building over many years. Criticisms of church life and practice had been growing over time, and what they might describe as the heyday, the pinnacle of their church experience and engagement in the church, was long since gone. How long should you stay in a church—ten, twenty, thirty years? At what point do things become stale, routine, perhaps exemplified in testimonies based on past, historical events and not the present day? Consequently, some resignations were undoubtedly a blessed relief for both sides, releasing some for a new experience of church which would hopefully be renewing for their faith.

RACIAL BIAS

As I previously explained, I was deeply saddened to lose from the church our first black elder. I greatly prized his place on the team and so there was a commensurate sense of loss when he stepped down and left the church. But throughout 2022, I continued to see his departure repeated amongst many of our non-white members, with the result that a disproportionate number of non-white members left the church. This included a young couple whom I had married just six months earlier. A random email asking whether I would be able to marry them led to a conversation and then the wedding, even though this was not their home church. But in that contact a relationship grew, and they began to attend church and participate in church life. It was great to have them around. But this issue concerned them and after a long conversation over a meal, they decided they should leave.

One exception to this trend was the visit of a representative of a Christian charity who came to the church one Sunday in May 2022 to update us on the work they were undertaking. After the service, as I was helping her pack up her stall, she questioned me about one of the notices I had given. "What is this Bible study you are doing about inclusion?" I explained the context and the process we were undertaking. She then shared how a friend of hers, another young, black Christian, with West African heritage, had taken his life—ostensibly, she thought, because his sexual orientation was not recognized or accepted within her community.

Whilst I respect the decisions that our non-white members had made as being considered and prayerful, I cannot but think that there was at least a significant cultural element to their decision. In South East Asia and Africa, especially West Africa, there is strong cultural opposition to same-sex relations, and it appeared that this too had its part to play in shaping how people responded to the issue. Looking back to what I said in chapter 3 about how we are all impacted by upbringing and culture, perhaps this should have been less of a surprise.

FINANCIAL HIT

With people leaving the church, there was a consequent decline in our income. Those with a more conservative theology were also likely to be those who understood and practiced a strong ethic around giving, and therefore losing these people meant there was a commensurate drop in revenue. This amounted to something around £6,000 per month or £70,000 p.a. Whilst ABC could be described as a wealthy church situated in an affluent area, in the years running up to 2022 we had been unusually blessed with some extraordinary levels of giving that had significantly boosted the church's reserves. Whilst we had agreed to give away a proportion of this and invest some in much-needed redevelopment of our Hub community building, this also meant that we had a buffer to smooth out the decline we were now experiencing. Perhaps we were beginning to understand why God had provided for us so generously over those years.

REPUTATIONAL IMPACT

We also had to face the fact that because LGBT+ inclusion appears to be for some in the church the defining feature of one's evangelical credentials, we were now known to be an inclusive church. ABC is a church which is reasonably well-known beyond its immediate vicinity. In part, that is because over the years it has drawn people from a wide geographic area and because it has been known for some remarkable missional initiatives. For good or ill, ABC had, or still has, "a reputation." This meant that the decision the church made became known widely, doubtless leaving some shaking their heads in dismay wondering, "But I never thought ABC was the kind of church which. . ." For some others, it will have been at least intriguing that ABC had come to this view, and for still others, it will have been a source of wonder and delight.

This reputational impact would obviously be focused upon me. Whereas other churches, especially local ones, might have previously considered me suitable to preach at their church on a Sunday, or lead a church weekend, this was now less likely. Whether or not I would be asked to speak about our process, the decision would be a signal to some that I was now *persona non grata*.

OVERSEAS MISSION

As with most churches, ABC has a significant and long-standing commitment to churches and organizations overseas. These grow and develop over time and are often strengthened through prayer, financial support, and mission trips to visit these partners. For twenty years, ABC has enjoyed a strong relationship with a Baptist church in Hungary, visiting annually to run and more recently help support, their annual children's holiday club. In 2022, a small team of six, of which I was a member, once again flew out to support this work. We had a fabulous week, running English classes, giving teaching input, holding a traditional English school sports day, and generally mucking in wherever we could. Once again, the team enjoyed the extraordinary hospitality of the church, and relationships were further strengthened.

There was next to no talk of the conversation ABC was having about inclusion, albeit that it was referenced in one home and the minister therefore did ask about what ABC was discussing. Wanting to explore some new ways to develop our relationship with the church in Hungary, we invited the minister to the UK to attend the annual Fresh Streams Conference. This would be something quite novel for him and we had hoped that it might be helpful exposure to a church leaders' conference which could perhaps inspire him with ideas he could instigate back in his own context.

At the conference in January 2023, only passing reference was made to LGBT+ inclusion and it wasn't until the car journey back from the conference that the minister asked me more about

ABC's discussions. This gave me the opportunity to explain the motivations for our discernment process, its content, and the possible conclusions to which we were moving. I referenced the fact that the following month the church would finally make its decision. He listened attentively and explained that his practice would be that when young people expressed same-sex attraction, a conversation with them elicited a consistent reason for this, a troubled upbringing. He said that an abusive or absent father, or coming under the influence of the wrong people, were the likely reasons for the same-sex attraction and so, with prayer and counselling, the young person would be delivered from such things. We didn't press each other further.

Spring is the time when discussions around our annual trip to Hungary would begin, but this time there would be a fly in the ointment. After our initial email asking about the holiday club, the pastor replied asking for details of the decision we had made on LGBT+ inclusion. I sent a full email, detailing the result and how it had come about, but it soon became apparent in the email exchange that this posed a difficulty for our ongoing relationship. By now we had both stayed in each other's homes and got to know each other's families; we had become friends. But having received my email, he explained that he now had to discuss the matter with his elders. The process stalled and finally the trip was cancelled.

I wondered whether, if we had been invited, there might have been new conditions for our involvement. However, we would most likely have done what we would always have done. We would have decided to respect the Hungarian church's view and if a young person raised the matter with us, we would have simply referred them back to the minister. Equally, what if we would have taken gay young people to be a part of our team and they had been challenged about their sexual orientation by a member of the Hungarian church? Email contact and a mutual understanding that there is more that unites us than divides us means that a relationship still exists between the two churches, but questions around how we might navigate having gay team members are now academic.

In these ways, and perhaps also in others yet unseen, we have needed to recognize the ways in which our view on this issue has impacted relationships, finances, reputation, and mission. Yet despite these dimensions of the cost we were paying, there were significant blessings we were beginning to experience as a result of becoming an inclusive church.

A NEW PLACE

Firstly, and quite simply, we had completed the process of discernment we had undertaken and were now enjoying clarity on the issue. The old tensions and anxieties around this issue were now gone. There was no longer any uncertainty or ambiguity about this issue, and as the church experienced a collective sigh of relief, we found that we had reached a happier, more unified, and peaceful place. Other churches and church leaders are understandably nervous about having the conversation we had, but such timidity can simply delay the fact that it will most probably have to take place at some point.

YOUNGER MEMBERS OF THE CHURCH

When talking to younger members of the church about the issue of LGBT+ inclusion, it had been our experience that they were almost universally in favor of it. For many of them, it seemed to be a "non-issue," so obvious to them and fundamental to how they behave and interact with others that it seemed antiquated and old-fashioned even to be considering otherwise. Admittedly, this view was unlikely to be the product of their searching the scriptures and coming to this conclusion, but more likely a product of their life-experience and the change in culture. In this respect I had previously challenged some of our young adults in the same way my mathematics teacher at school had challenged me: "Ashley, you may have the right answer but show me your working!" Showing "working" was not something I was readily provided with by the young people.

Whilst not being a reason to pursue the process, the decision we made has brought about a greater resonance between young people and the faith we espouse, something which did not previously exist. The decision might, in the minds of some young people, also help to remove this obstacle to faith and in part address the decline in church involvement we have seen over recent decades.

"SO RUN ME THROUGH THIS. . ."

For a limited time after the decision, ABC also seemed to become the go-to place to understand how to take a church through such a process. The leadership teams of several churches in the north of England contacted me to ask whether we could meet, so they could hear about the discernment process we had undertaken. In addition, a Baptist theological college was also in contact about what we had done, and I spent several hours on Zoom talking with two lecturers who were planning a similar conversation with their students. So, for a while at least, we became a repository of some wisdom on the matter.

ATTRACTIONAL TO PEOPLE

As much as we have seen numbers of people leave the church, making this decision has also become a reason to join the church. On hearing that the church was about to make a decision about LGBT+ inclusion, two recent regular attenders keen to support such a move asked to become members to participate in the process and decision-making. Also, after the decision was made, a regular attender of some five years decided that they would become a member because the church had now made a decision which, in their eyes, was fundamental to the church they would wish to join.

ALL HEAVEN BROKE LOOSE

During 2022, I had spoken with or met other Baptist church leaders who had undertaken this process in their own churches. It was of enormous help to listen to and quiz those who had already walked this path to gain insight and understanding. Although it was not an aspect of the conversation which I had expected, these church leaders seemed to add the same postscript to the story they told me. They said, "Oh and by the way, it's had the most incredible impact across the whole life of the church. We have become so welcoming to everybody and relations across the church are so strong and supportive."

When I heard this, my instinctive reaction had been to celebrate the shift they had experienced, but equally I felt that this was an experience unique to their situation. I was carrying the weight of the process, knowing the sharp criticisms and sad departures which defined our journey, and part of my hope was simply an ending of these burdens. But I was wrong (again). In the weeks that followed the 9th of February, a tenor of welcome, worshipfulness, joy, and release was detonated across the church.

Perhaps we just relaxed! Or perhaps it happened simply because those who were opposed to the decision had left, with the result that the breadth of opinion on LGBT+ inclusion had narrowed, leaving a more homogeneous group of people. Yet these explanations still seem inadequate. There does appear to be something about this issue, something about throwing off the shackles and restraints of a more judgmental and legalistic culture and fully embracing a way of following Jesus, that does not discriminate, that doesn't judge or compare, which meant that we were enjoying more of the kingdom life that the church should always have known.

REMOVING BARRIERS

On Sunday 12th February, just three days after making our decision, we shared communion. I know that in many Baptist churches the serving of communion is reserved for the elders or deacons, or at least those who have been pre-requested to do so. But it has been my practice for some time to invite, at this point in the service, any who felt prompted to serve. I think it is a grace which blesses people and perhaps confirms any prompting that the Spirit might be making during the service.

On this particular Sunday, I made the same invitation to come and serve, and saw some people stand and move to the front. Among them, I watched a man of West African heritage get up and also move to the front. The thing was, I had never seen this man before that morning. As I handed out the bread to those serving, I turned and quietly welcomed him, introducing myself as I handed him the bread, then off he went to serve bread and wine as dutifully and respectfully as all the others. It wasn't until after the service that I got to meet him properly. Only then did I discover his name and that he was attending church with his wife and daughters. He was born in Nigeria, had grown up in the Roman Catholic Church, but hadn't attended a church for at least five years. He lived a few doors down from the church and had felt prompted to attend. I sensed joy and a deep peace about having this new family with us, and about his response and involvement.

Also, around this time, a local hotel had been taken over by the Home Office to house around 140 asylum seekers from more than twenty different nationalities. Our community-focused work in The Hub serving those who are especially lonely, or in debt, or struggling with the cost of living, or are asylum seekers, meant that, in association with other local churches, we quickly made contact with them, and not only did they attend our weekly community meal and a range of other activities, but some came on a Sunday. Hurriedly we began to learn new languages, not just to speak, but new languages of hospitality and friendship. Bible readings were now given in Farsi, Spanish or Portuguese as well as English, and sermons were translated and distributed to make that aspect of services more comprehensible.

Further to this, and quite coincidentally, we had a couple of unplanned changes to our services. We are blessed as a church by having some people with neurodiversity as a part of our family. This includes two autistic young men. In those weeks after the decision, we happened to have some "open mic" aspects to our services and at each of them, one of the autistic young men felt able to participate and share. Then at a communion service, as I was standing at the table, one of them, a seventeen year old, came and stood by me. As I read some words and introduced this part of the service, he raised his hand and gently began to rub my head (much to my wife's amusement). He then asked if he could say something and so I handed him the mic. He shared his experience of having autism and how it impacted his life. After a few minutes, and thinking that we should probably move on, I asked the rhetorical question as to whether I could have the mic back. Given that with autism there are no rhetorical questions, he stated "Yes, you can have the mic back." I prayed and communion was served. He wanted to be involved, included, and he was.

We were now a Baptist church where, if you were seeking asylum and from a different country and even faith background, were neurodiverse with a different take on the world, or were from a Roman Catholic background and had not been to church for a long time, you could attend, sense God's prompting, and feel part of what was happening. You could take part in the service or even take a role in serving communion, despite the practice being alien to you or whether you knew those you were serving or not. I cannot overstress what a joy it had been to observe these things happening.

Personally, I felt as if a great weight had been lifted off my shoulders and I was granted new permission and freedom to express myself in worship, teaching, preaching, and service leading. The sung-worship life of the church seemed to expand and grow. There was greater freedom of expression, and the church sounded as if we were singing with one voice. The practical work of ministry, coordinating the church staff team and determining outcomes at elders' meetings, were all now characterized by a lightness, winsomeness, and joy we had not previously known. As much as I might try to define exactly why this is the case, it seems beyond human manufacture and was a consequence of the Spirit's work in us. In short, it felt like all heaven had been let loose.

Finally, I want to refer to those who had opposed the decision that the church had made, but who decided to remain in the church. This was undoubtedly a hard and costly choice, even though the church almost unanimously approved the proposal to "commit ourselves to living graciously together in the community of Christ regardless of differences on these matters. . ." One person said to me that, despite the decision, this was "their church" and they were not about to walk away from it. Others took a pragmatic view that this was just one aspect of the church and we remained united by our core convictions. Some others were still weighing up what they thought. Those who stayed felt that, although we had disagreed, we had disagreed well, and they were unlikely to experience a level of antipathy towards them which would drive them from the church. On the contrary, ABC still felt like a safe place to be.

On reflection, I realize that we were yet to experience the final denouement, the full outworking of our decision in church life. Would it mean that we hung Pride flags outside the church, or detail our new inclusivity on the noticeboard? Would we, as some churches have done, start attending Manchester Pride as a regular church activity? The first step would be to detail our new identity on the front page of our website to make it clear to everyone the level of inclusion we now offer. The statement read:

> We welcome people of all ages, genders, ethnicities, gender identities, sexual orientations, physical and mental abilities, neurodiversities, education, classes, economic status, or political outlook.

As we began to enjoy the new world we were experiencing, we also had time to reflect.

11

Reflecting on the Process

IN TALKING TO CHURCH leaders about the discernment process, I am asked the repeated question as to whether, on reflection, I would have done anything differently. To which my answer is always, perhaps annoyingly, "Yes—and no."

"Yes," because the process undertaken must be tailored to the church. If you are genuinely seeking to engage the whole church family in discernment, then you must include not only the people, but the church's culture and history as well. You will have seen how, for us, a particular set of circumstances precipitated the decision of the elders to have the conversation. That meant factoring in our evangelical identity, the pastoral matters we were engaging with, and our Baptist identity and practice. Also, the conversation had been delayed for a period because of the need to settle ourselves after the Covid-19 pandemic.

But I would also say "No," because we took such care through the process to recognize and respond to what was happening at each stage. This is obviously a subjective view, and I am aware of those who struggled with the discernment or left the church, who may well posit an alternative view. But the outcome might give some veracity to the idea that we explored the issue thoroughly, with care and always listening to the Spirit, and finally discerned together as a congregation.

Of course, the success of the process was not simply down to me or the elders. The church family was tested and put in a position we had not previously experienced. There were some difficult conversations and perhaps even harder, some views expressed in ways which seemed designed to attack, obstruct, or subvert the process. However, these were the minority. The overwhelming majority of church family members were able to listen, hear, and hold the difference. They understood the need to have this conversation and were secure and open to what they might find. They were also able to draw back from the idea, proposed by some, that this issue was the true determinant of evangelical orthodoxy. I am therefore immensely proud of the church family and how they conducted themselves. Irrespective of the outcome, they were prayerful, diligent in study and acted with great grace and love towards one another.

A further reflection would have to be, and I hadn't realized this at first, that the process was about more than LGBT+ inclusion. As you read in the previous chapter, the outcomes were many and varied. I had thought that the issue might be addressed in "splendid isolation." Just as we had previously revisited the issue of lottery funding, or who could become a member, I had wrongly assumed that by examining our understanding of LGBT+ inclusion, we would do just that—come to a mind on just this issue. But we didn't, because it turned out to be far broader than that.

The 2014 British film *Pride* is based upon the true story of how a group of lesbian and gay activists in London ended up fundraising and supporting the Welsh families affected by the 1984 miners' strike. Although seemingly disparate, they found a common cause. Similarly, in reaching out to include those from the LGBT+ communities, we discovered the imperative to reach out to all people and learned new dimensions of love, welcome, acceptance, and inclusion. This I never foresaw, yet it has brought a wonderful richness to our church life and brought greater glory to God.

Postscript

A MONTH AFTER WE had made our decision, I was forwarded an email from the church administrator. This was not in itself unusual; lots of emails are sent to the church's generic contact address, which are then forwarded by the admin team to whoever is best placed to answer the message. But this one was different. It was odd, a random "To whom it may concern" kind of email, which made a strange, yet intriguing request.

It was from True North, a television production company, and briefly explained that a cast member on one of their reality shows wanted to get baptized, and they were asking whether we could do it. I'm not sure how other ministers or church leaders might respond to such an email, or indeed how you are supposed to respond. Initially I let out a sigh, with thoughts akin to, "Really? I mean, what do they think the church is, just a means to facilitate some dubious plotline? After all, what faith does this person have, if they were asking the production company to arrange this sacred rite for them?" Also, in almost thirty years of ministry, I had experienced a few brushes with the media, and in almost all of them I had been left feeling bruised.

I recalled that in the past I had received a similarly random request. It was to perform a wedding on the center spot at Odsal Stadium, home of the Bradford Bulls. I rang the bride-to-be and gently explained that I wasn't the person to do this. I also remembered a blog post from the wonderful Gordon Atkinson, aka "Real Live Preacher," who was asked to marry a couple in a picturesque white, weather-boarded, ex-chapel-turned-gallery. He said how he was taken aback by their request to leave out "the religious stuff," but was staggered even further when, having explained that "the religious stuff" was very much why he did weddings, that they hurriedly backtracked and said, "No, it's fine, really. You can leave the religious stuff in." Was it all so meaningless?

But I simply couldn't delete the email or decline the invitation. Within me there is a significant internal narrative which says that I am painfully aware of the reputation of the church in the world, and I didn't want this request to further add to society's dim view of Christian faith and the church. It may cost me some time and effort, and there was perhaps likely to be some awkwardness in speaking to the cast member, but I'll do it to leave as good an impression of the church as I could. I rang Gareth, the author of the email. To add complication to the issue, or at least to the way I was thinking, Gareth told me that the program was called *Teen Mom UK*, the UK iteration of a show originating from the States, and that the cast member in question was called "Sassi" and that she wanted a "full-body baptism." (More sighs on my part.)

Computing the aspects of this invitation, it seemed clear that there was only one way this could go. There would be a meeting with Sassi where I would listen to her story, ask about the motivation for her request and then somehow find the words to carefully, but clearly, explain why I couldn't do this. Of course, I'd do it without exactly saying, "This is not really the kind of baptism I do." But come on, who in their right mind would do this? As concerned as I was for the reputation of the church, this was eclipsed by my desire not to see this sacred act and the trinitarian God in whose name I would be baptizing, belittled by being party to this. (Also, a bit of me thought, "What would people think of me?")

Ten days later I met Sassi; in fact, I met Sassi and her sister. They came into the church office where, after some slightly awkward "hellos," we sat down in the meeting room to talk. I briefly explained a bit about me, the church and, with an enquiring smile, asked, "'So, you are thinking about getting baptized?" All the time my mind was thinking through how to get out of this situation in the most honoring way. Then Sassi told me her story. . ..

Sassi was Roman Catholic, brought up in the church which she still attended weekly with her daughter. She explained that she believed in God and how much her faith meant to her, which is why the next part of the story began to undo my defenses. Although a Christian, Sassi had recently had a wobble in her faith; perhaps "a wobble" was putting it mildly. She had decided that she would explore New Age religion and had booked herself in for a retreat in Wales. It had not gone well. She described her experience as being "dark"—far from the enlightening experience she had hoped for, and it had left her feeling sullied, contaminated by the episode. This was why she wanted to be baptized, to be made clean, to be cleansed, she said. She kept using that word, "cleansed."

I asked about the Roman Catholic church she attended, and she explained that of course, a full-body baptism like this, as a believer, was not something they would offer. She had been baptized as a baby and confirmed as a young person, but now that this had happened, she was looking beyond the church she knew so that she could be. . . cleansed. By this point my mind was working hard, like a satnav "recalculating" once a journey had taken an unforeseen turn. I was now inputting a set of wholly different data and working hard to establish the possible new destination. To buy some time, I asked about her priest. Sassi had spoken to him and he wasn't especially happy with her idea. It obviously fell outside the normal and acceptable practices for Catholics. I realized that if I was to be involved, it would be respectful to speak to him, explaining that as much as this was an ecclesiological "no-no" for him, I was just as clear of the opinion that this was appropriate. So, there I was, already talking myself into taking part in this crazy reality TV baptism for Catholic teen mom, Sassi. Or perhaps this was something else. Perhaps Sassi was my modern-day Mary Magdalene who, despite seeming unsuitable, just wanted to show her devotion to Jesus. Who was I to deny her that?

We prayed. I prayed, especially for her to be delivered from any darkness or hold that her time away in Wales might still have on her. I prayed for her to be filled with God's Holy Spirit, his Spirit who can cleanse and heal, who delights in her and whose love for her is beyond her wildest imaginings. And I prayed about the day when I would likely baptize her.

You don't really need to know much more of the story. We set a date—a Sunday afternoon a month or so later. I did try to speak to her priest, but he either wasn't available or was away on pilgrimage. When the afternoon came, we gathered. There were six or seven TV people, Sassi, her close family and friends, and about thirty came from ABC, simply to support and encourage her. Once the TV stuff was finally set, our two worship leaders struck up and in a moment the atmosphere was transformed. The church sang worshipfully, beautifully, just as they had in the main service that morning; I was so grateful and proud of them.

Sassi and I sat on the edge of the stage, and I asked questions which might elicit her story, her testimony. Her mum and I then stepped into the water, and we baptized Sassi together, the strangeness and wonder of baptism striking me afresh. Once changed, we stood together at the front and I invited members of the church to come and pray for her, prophesy over her—and they did. With great love and care, they looked her in the eye and spoke words of faith and grace over her life and future. There seemed no less holiness in this filmed moment than in any other baptism I had performed, and I knew it would touch each person present. As something of a confirmation of this, as we cleared away later, a crew member would come and talk to me about his early years of faith, growing up with a vicar for a father.

Why am I telling you this? After all, it's not a story about the LGBT+ communities and how we now include them. I tell you because this is a story about listening to a person and finding resonance between their story and the story of the Bible. It's a story about addressing personal prejudice and assumptions, and then daring to break with convention in order to do the good and godly thing. And I tell you this, because while I was standing there listening to my brilliant congregation pray over her, I sensed God saying to me, "Ash, given all you have learned in the past year, I think I can now trust you and the church to do the right thing by a Roman Catholic, teen mom and reality TV star called Sassi."

Bibliography

Baptists Together. "Declaration of Principal," https://www.baptist.org.uk/Groups/220595/Declaration_of_Principle.aspx

Bebbington, David. W. *Evangelicalism in Modern Britain: a history from the 1730's to the 1980's*, London: Routledge, 1995

Brueggeman, Walter. *Virus as a Summons to Faith : Biblical Reflections in a Time of Loss, Grief and Uncertainty*, Milton Keynes: Pasternoster, 2020

Derry, C. "Lesbianism and the criminal law of England and Wales." https://www.open.edu/openlearn/society-politics-law/law/lesbianism-and-the-criminal-law-england-and-wales

DeYoung, Kevin. *What does the Bible Really Teach About Homosexuality?* London: IVP, 2015

Elmes, Stephen. *Sexuality, Faith, & the Art of Conversation: Part One*, Bookham: Creative Tension, 2017

Elmes, Stephen. *Sexuality, Faith & the Art of Conversation: Parts Two, Three & Four*, Bookham: Creative Tension, 2019

Elmes, Stephen. *A Beautiful Endeavour: Pursuing a Conversation About Same-Sex Attraction and Following Jesus (Sexuality, Faith & the Art of Conversation)*, Bookham: Creative Tension, 2019

Fiddes et al. "Something to Declare," https://www.baptist.org.uk/Articles/366068/Something_to_Declare.aspx

Frost, Mike. "Breaking Up the Family in the Pursuit of Uniformity." https://mikefrost.net/breaking-up-the-family-in-the-pursuit-of-uniformity/

Gushee, David, P. *Changing Our Mind*. Canton: Read the Spirit, 2017

Haley Barton, Ruth. *Strengthening the Soul of Your Leadership*, Downers Grove: IVP, 2008 PP

Haley Barton, Ruth. *Pursuing God's Will Together, A Discernment Practice for Leadership Groups*, Downers Grove: IVP, 2012 63–64, 219

Helminiak, Daniel A. *What the Bible Really Says About Homosexuality*, Kindle Scribe, 2000

Himbaza, Innocent. Schenker, Adrien. Edart, Jean-Baptiste. *The Bible on the Question of Homosexuality*. Washington: Catholic University American, 2012

Bibliography

Lencioni, Patrick. *The Five Dysfunctions of a Team*, Hoboken: John Wiley & Sons, 2002

Lennox, John, C. *Where is God in a Coronavirus World?*, Epsom: Good Book Company, 2020

Loader, DeFranza, et al. *Two Views on Homosexuality, the Bible, and the Church*, Grand Rapids: Zondervan, 2016

Murray, Stuart. *The Church After Christendom*. Milton Keynes: Authentic, 2005

Patten, Malcolm. *Leading a Multicultural Church*. London: SPCK, 2016

Peacock, Gavin. Strachan, Owen. *What Does the Bible Teach about Homosexuality?: A Short Book on Biblical Sexuality (Sexuality And Identity)*. Tain: Christian Focus, 2020

Rogers, Jack. *Jesus, the Bible, and Homosexuality*. Louisville: Westminster John Knox, 2009

Shaw, Ed. *The Plausibility Problem*. London: Inter-Varsity Press, 2015

Wolfenden, John, et al. "Report of the Committee on Homosexual Offences and Prostitution," https://www.humandignitytrust.org/wp-content/uploads/resources/Wolfenden_Report_1957.pdf

Willett, G. T. "Archbishops Fisher and Ramsey, and the Wolfenden report," https://www.churchtimes.co.uk/articles/2006/3-november/comment/letters-to-the-editor/archbishops-fisher-and-ramsey-and-the-wolfenden-report

World Evangelical Alliance. "Statement of Faith," https://worldea.org/who-we-are/statement-of-faith/

Wright, N. T. *God and the Pandemic: A Christian Reflection on the Coronavirus and it's Aftermath*. Grand Rapids: Zondervan, 2020

Milton Keynes UK
Ingram Content Group UK Ltd.
UKHW050302030924
447802UK00007B/515

9 798385 213948